CENTRAL PARK

Coach: 25 Writers Reflect on People
Who Made a Difference
Brothers: 26 Stories of Love and Rivalry
Anatomy of Baseball (with Lee Gutkind)

CENTRAL PARK

An Anthology

Edited by
Andrew Blauner

BLOOMSBURY

New York   Berlin   London   Sydney

LIBRARY OF CONGRESS CATALOGING-IN-PUBLICATION DATA

Central Park : an anthology / edited by Andrew Blauner.—1st U.S. ed.
p. cm.
ISBN-13: 978-1-60819-600-5 (pbk.)
ISBN-10: 1-60819-600-3 (pbk.)
1. Central Park (New York, N.Y.) 2. Central Park
(New York, N.Y.)—Anecdotes. I. Blauner, Andrew.
F128.65.C3C27 2012
974.7'1—dc23
2011042204

First U.S. Edition 2012

3 5 7 9 10 8 6 4

Typeset by Westchester Book Group
Printed in the U.S.A. by Quad/Graphics, Fairfield, Pennsylvania

"Central Park was once my Eden."
—James Salter

CONTENTS

CONTENTS

CENTRAL PARK

ADRIAN BENEPE
Introduction

I RECENTLY HAD the opportunity to record an oral history of New York City's parks for a high-tech start-up. The software wizards there created a Web-based map of the world and asked people near and far—comedians, bartenders, professors, city servants—to talk about their pieces of the world. Mine involves approximately five thousand pieces of property under the jurisdiction of the NYC Department of Parks & Recreation, our parks, playgrounds, beaches, recreation facilities, meadows, and woodlands covering more than twenty-nine thousand acres, about 14 percent of the city. Yet I found myself telling not one, not two, but three tales of Central Park. The first described a few of the park's quirky characters, the second discussed the amazing temporary art installation known as *The Gates*, and the third covered the great statues and monuments featured along Literary Walk and throughout the park's great expanse.

* * *

When I was in college, I had a summer job, perhaps my most interesting summer job, as a pushcart vendor in Central Park. It was an enormous pushcart that belonged to the Front Porch restaurant on the West Side of Manhattan. This was in the summer of 1976, the summer of the Bicentennial celebration, the tall ships, and fireworks, when disco was ascendant and *A Chorus Line* opened on Broadway. It was a summer when NYC was mostly grimy and decrepit, with stifling subway cars covered in graffiti, but there were signs that all was not lost. It was also a summer when a girl I had just met at Middlebury College came to visit from her home in California, and Charlotte Glasser fell in love with New York, and would later marry me in Central Park.

Every day, I would get my cart and fill it up with tureens of cold soup and interesting fruit breads and push it—all six hundred pounds of it—from West Eighty-second Street to Fifty-ninth Street. I sold food at lunchtime at the south end of the park, and then, after lunch, I pushed the cart to the Delacorte Theater, outside of which I sold food at dinnertime. Though the cart lacked a Parks permit and the restaurant did not inform me that I needed one, no one enforced the rules at the time. There was a passel of other vendors selling creative food, and a few classic hot dog/ pretzel guys who likely had real permits. Every once in a while a police officer would show up and shoo us away, but we would come back and sell our soup, falafel, or tacos. (The charismatic guy who sold falafel would shout out to prospective customers, "Falafel—Will Not Make You Feel . . . Awful!") We banded together and enjoyed friendly competition, except for the two hot dog guys, who once had a fight that ended with one stabbing the other in his arm with a large hot dog fork. During this time, I came to know a lot of the people who seem slightly unreal to me now.

When we refer to the "bad old days" of Central Park, we are usually talking about the days of rampant crime, graffiti, abandoned buildings, bare lawns, and dead trees. And yet I miss some aspects of those old days. In particular, Central Park was home to a lot of "characters" who added to the atmosphere, but who, for the most part, are not there anymore.

One of the characters I met, the Poet O, trundled around Central Park with a shopping cart. He had a bushy white beard and he would ring a handbell. If you gave him money, he thanked you by reciting a poem that he composed on the spot, a sort of blank verse. He made promises to cure paying listeners of sexual diseases by ringing his bell. I talked with him often, and once he realized that I didn't have the means to pay him for his wisdom, he dispensed it for free. Among other things, he explained to me the value of Central Park as a large, outdoor sanitorium. He said he was mentally ill, and the park enabled him to get out of his single room in a West Side hotel and be out in nature—not elbow to elbow with people—where he could experience what he called "the natural medication of nature." The park, he explained, was saving the government huge amounts of money by allowing mentally ill people to "self-medicate" through the intoxicants of the romantic landscape and avoid expensive mental hospitals and drugs.

Another character, a flamboyant man with a pompadour, toured the park on an elaborate bicycle, pulling a tricycle with a red wagon behind it. A series of enormous tropical birds, cockatoos and parrots, rode on the tricycle and wagon behind him as he circled the park, allowing people to admire his birds.

Perhaps the best known was Adam Purple, with his long flowing white beard and purple, tie-dyed clothes, who traveled the park on his purple bicycle picking up horse manure to compost in his garden on the Lower East Side. For a while, a woman in purple, whom he called Eve, accompanied him.

A hippie named "Mountain," who had long, dirty-blond hair, played Frisbee every day by the Naumburg Bandshell. The Bandshell was where the other hippie kids hung out. Mountain, not one of the rich kids from Central Park West or Fifth Avenue, was lean and muscular and had the air of a Westie from Hell's Kitchen. He knew how to throw a Frisbee better than anyone else and served as a kind of Peter Pan leader of the Lost Boys (and girls) of that generation. But Frisbee wasn't his only talent. Mountain could commune with anyone, and he had to, because the area was habituated not only by middle- and upper-class teenagers, but also by a group of drug dealers who counted on the kids as customers. Soon enough, a new group would overtake the area—roller disco skaters in colorful outfits dancing to Donna Summer's "Love to Love You Baby," and then, in another summer, Chic singing "Le Freak" as dozens of skaters and hundreds of onlookers of all races and nationalities and sexual persuasions grooved and mingled and proved why New York City was the capital of where people just got along.

These were some of the Central Park characters. Today, they are not nearly as numerous. The Central Park Conservancy and New York City have invested six hundred million dollars in private and public funds to restore the glory of the nineteenth-century landscape in a way that suits twenty-first-century users. Ladies in hoop skirts and gentlemen in linen suits strolling along the paths have given way to both genders running and cycling in Lycra tops and bottoms that their predecessors would have seen as underwear. Or perhaps you simply cannot see the characters now that almost forty million visitors enter the park each year. I suppose it is better that the park is busier than ever rather than abandoned, which it essentially was back in the seventies. Maybe now you just have to look a little closer to find the characters.

For sixteen days in February 2005, Central Park was transformed by the now-famous art installation known as *The Gates*. Centuries of great sculptors are featured along Literary Walk and throughout the park's broad expanse, and *The Gates*, like a powerful orange highlighter, drew the attention of millions of New Yorkers for a blissful and brief rapprochement with the unexpected and the great.

The NYC park system has a very large temporary art program. The Parks Department works with groups like the Public Art Fund and Creative Time and also with independent artists to temporarily install contemporary works in parks across the city, notably on Park Avenue and at Grand Army Plaza and in City Hall Park, among many other places. I became deeply involved in perhaps the greatest and briefest exhibit, *The Gates,* by Christo and Jeanne-Claude, in the early 2000s. Mayor Michael Bloomberg thought the project would have merit both as a work of art and as a tourist draw, so he and Deputy Mayor Patti Harris instructed me to ensure the park's safety first, but ultimately to try make the idea a reality.

Over the previous twenty-five years, we had repeatedly informed Christo and Jeanne-Claude why we could not allow them to do the project. In its initial version, the plan called for fifteen thousand gates, with footings deep in the lawns, rocks, and woodlands of the park, and an autumn installation date. With so much potential damage to the park at stake, and scheduled as it originally was at a time of high visitation (and bird migration), as well as staunch opposition from preservationists and community residents, their project seemed undoable. In fact, Park Commissioners Gordon Davis and Henry Stern both formally turned it down, in Davis's case with an elaborately argued booklet of more than hundred pages.

Now it was my job to try to find a way to make it work, and Central Park Administrator Doug Blonsky and I, along with a very diplomatic assistant parks commissioner named

Jack Linn, had the task of figuring out how to work with the artists so they could realize their extremely personal vision while doing no damage to the park's landscape nor unduly disturbing the resident wildlife and park visitors. The artists had to figure out a way—and they did very cleverly with their engineer, Vince Davenport—to construct *The Gates* without digging holes in the park. Among the many ingenious aspects of their design was the use of hollow, extruded vinyl tubing to be used for the gates themselves, an idea based on similar technology used for fencing horse paddocks. The design used heavy weights to which lightweight gates were bolted to the asphalt paths. Christo and Jeanne-Claude also reduced the number of gates by half and installed the exhibit in February, during the park's icy season, when visitation is normally extremely low and no bird migration takes place. The artists, along with Vince and his wife, Jonita, organized an army of paid technicians and volunteers to install the gates, and the entire process, including countless technical meetings, public review presentations, press conferences, and walks through the park, were part of the work of art. By the project's conclusion, the park remained completely unharmed.

On February 12, 2005, Mayor Bloomberg and the artists unfurled one of the saffron-colored curtains overhead, the crowds streamed through, and like a very long line of dominoes, the other gates were unfurled by volunteers. *The Gates* went up for sixteen extraordinary days during which time something like two million people visited Central Park in the year's coldest month. It was a transformative experience for me. I had gone from being the guy who had to deliver the bad news as to why the show could *not* go on in the nineties, to being the one who helped make it happen. *The Gates* made me, and millions of visitors, look anew at Central Park, because the rows of orange gates formed lines across the landscape, undulating with the terrain, sweeping up and down hills, and swooping along lake edges and roadways, as if a giant hand had traced the contours of the park with an orange highlighter. For the first and perhaps only time, the complexity of this work of art, designed by Frederick Law Olmsted and Calvert Vaux in the 1850s, was dissected and revealed in a way it had never been before, brilliant but evanescent. People thronged into the park and packed nearby hotels, shops, and restaurants; it was even rumored that the Starbucks near Columbus Circle ran out of cups. Tourism hit record numbers, and the city saw a positive economic impact estimated at almost $250 million. Like the three days of peace and love at Woodstock in 1969, the two weeks of unbridled joy in New York City in 2005 touched even the most cynical of the city's residents. Perhaps most important, New Yorkers felt a very tangible sense that they could recover from the terrible devastation of the World Trade Center attacks. *The Gates* was not just the single greatest art installation the city has ever enjoyed; it was a reaffirmation of the enduring vitality of New York City and cities in general.

In the seventies, Central Park was a municipal embarrassment and a symbol of a city going down the tubes in a hurry.

Graffiti obscured everything in sight, including the abandoned, once-historic buildings, festooned with extraordinary ornamentation, designed by eminent architects of the previous century. Vandals broke off pieces of stone carvings on the Bethesda Terrace. The fountains were empty and full of scrawl. The rowboats were covered with graffiti. There was no grass on the lawns, and the park lacked horticulture. The poorest of people made overnight homes in the burned-out buildings. Crime soared, from rampant drug dealing to hundreds of muggings and even murders. That was Central Park, the city's premier park; one can imagine what the rest of the park system looked like.

These were the parks I knew as a teenager, in the summer of 1973 when I first worked for the Parks Department on the Lower East Side, cleaning toilets and locker rooms at the Dry Dock Pool on East Tenth Street and then picking up garbage and sweeping up huge piles of beer cans in the East River Park. I learned firsthand that a combination of reduced funding, low morale, and poor work attitudes can drive even a once proud park system to its lowest level. It was also the Central Park I first encountered when I graduated from Middlebury College and came back to New York City in the early spring of 1979.

Through a series of happy accidents, I made my way to the Parks Department, meeting Betsy Barlow, the newly appointed Central Park administrator, while working as an unpaid intern at a community newspaper. I learned about Commissioner Gordon Davis's wonderful idea to start a program called the "Urban Park Rangers." The Rangers would bring a corps of fresh-faced, mostly young and idealistic parks "ambassadors" to the public and show in a tangible way that the park system was undergoing a rebirth under Mayor Ed Koch. From May 1979 to September 1980 I served as an Urban Park Ranger. On one of my first patrols, walking through the Ramble, I stopped to talk to a middle-aged man, who said, "You know, I've lived in New York all my life, and the city really got lost when we abandoned the parks to the vandals and the hooligans." He told me, "When we gave away the parks to the bad guys, that was the end of the city." And I think he said, or he may simply have implied that "we will take back the city, and the city will become livable again, when the parks feel safe and decent again."

It was very hard to feel hopeful about the future at that time. I would look at tinted postcards and black-and-white photos of old Central Park with perfect green lawns and flowers and fences and intact buildings and monuments and no graffiti and say, "Look at the terrible things that have happened. Can it ever be nice again?"

Soon, the city, and its parks, did indeed begin to become "nice again." The Central Park Conservancy was formed under the leadership of Betsy Barlow, who was named park administrator by Mayor Koch and Commissioner Davis. The city restored the Sheep Meadow, and the Dairy was reopened as a visitor center. Then came the magnificent restorations of the Belvedere Castle in Central Park and the Boathouse in Prospect Park. Each time a restoration occurred, the city sent a message. It was like winning a war against decrepitude and vandalism and all the bad things that had happened. With some minor bumps along the way, the work started by Davis and Koch and continued under Mayors David Dinkins and Rudy Giuliani and their respective parks commissioners, Betsy Gotbaum and Henry Stern, paved the way for Mayor Bloomberg to lead the largest expansion and improvement of the park system since the halcyon days of the WPA and Robert Moses.

The NYC Parks Department, among many other things, oversees most of the city's collection of statues and monuments; certainly everything that is in a park. Statues and monuments in a city are traditions that go back to the ancient days of Egypt, Rome, and Greece. The primary purpose of civic sculptures and monuments in the nineteenth and twentieth centuries was to honor heroes or ideals. Parks have memorials to all of the wars; to generals, soldiers, presidents, and other leaders. There are bronze statues and generals on horseback (unfortunately, all men). More recent additions to New York City parks include statues of Eleanor Roosevelt, Gertrude Stein, and Harriet Tubman, as well as those representing a diversity of backgrounds—Mahatma Gandhi and Duke Ellington and Frederick Douglass, among others.

Some of the very best sculptors lived and practiced here in New York City. Augustus Saint-Gaudens, a man many consider the best sculptor of the nineteenth century, and certainly the best American sculptor ever and a true genius, was born and raised on East Twenty-second Street.

Before becoming a successful sculptor, he served as a cameo cutter and then an apprentice.

He eventually relocated to Cornish, New Hampshire, and founded the Cornish Colony, where all the artists and writers and sculptors and painters—including John Singer Sargent—went and lived. He created some of the great sculptures of American history, including the one of Admiral David Farragut that stands in Madison Square Park, the seated figure of Peter Cooper that sits in a small triangle behind the Cooper Union, and perhaps most famously, the gilded statue of General William Tecumseh Sherman being led by the allegorical figure of Victory, which stands at Grand Army Plaza at Fifty-ninth Street and Fifth Avenue.

Today, Central Park is home to many statues and monuments, but very few have been added since the mid-twentieth century, when a trio of South American heroes went up along Central Park South. People now have come to understand that Central Park itself is, as the Central Park Conservancy historian and photographer Sara Cedar Miller stated, "the most important work of American art of the nineteenth century." Even more remarkably, it is a work of art that has managed to survive and evolve, look better than ever, and serve more visitors than ever, over 150 years after it was conceived and created. And it was considered perfect then.

Reading this volume is a little like a walk in the park with some truly excellent companions. It is a long distance, in a Proustian way, from the characters of Central Park I met then. But it underscores the fact that Central Park is not simply a geographic destination, nor just the essential masterpiece of landscape architecture and great creative accomplishment of the nineteenth century. Once you add people and time, it becomes an ever-evolving work of art and performance art. It is central to our thinking, our style, and our magnificence.

JOHN BURNHAM SCHWARTZ
The Meadow

H EADING SOUTH, THE lead runners of the 2009 New York City Marathon began to pass the Mount Sinai Kravis Children's Hospital on Fifth Avenue and Ninety-ninth Street at around nine thirty that Sunday morning. And my three-and-a-half-year-old son, his face pressed up against the window of the fifth-floor room in which he'd been trapped for several days, asked who was chasing the men, and why.

I was standing behind him, making sure he was well balanced and safe atop the radiator cover that ran the length of the window overlooking Central Park. I proceeded to tell him, at length, about marathons and the first Olympics, about the javelin and the discus and the triple jump. (My wife and I had been in that room with him all weekend, sleeping on chairs, watching his fever too slowly descend from its peak of 105, and more than likely I was a bit deranged.) As I spoke, on upper Fifth Avenue runners began to appear in freakish numbers. It was a human spectacle, eccentric and heroic both. We saw a female jogger dressed in a full-length chicken suit ("rooster," my son said) and a man with a bad limp pushing a disabled girl in a wheelchair. A light rain was falling, but, after twenty-two miles or so, no one seemed to notice. The boisterous crowds on either side of the street had grown in bacterial clusters, spontaneous ecosystems of friends, relatives, co-workers. Some generous soul was handing out Egg McMuffins—first come, first served. And high above in our sanitized room I stood with my fingers curled around my son's balsa-wood wrists, my unshaven chin scratching the top of his head. According to the doctors, the critical period of his still-undiagnosed virus was past; earlier that morning, in a kind of anticeremony, a nurse had removed his IV.

Set loose by relief and exhaustion, dazed by the endless parade, my mind began to wander. It air-walked across Fifth Avenue like Philippe Petit and slipped over the dark stone perimeter wall of the East Meadow—or, simply, the Meadow, as I'd once known it (as if there could be no other). To my right was a playground I did not remember. I crossed the paved footpath and strolled beneath the two towering American elms that stood sentry there, and out onto the acres-wide expanse of dirt field. It was the first of November, the ground mapped by footprints brimming with mud. Making my way across, I stepped carefully, avoiding landmines real and imagined. Ever since childhood I had perversely believed the park here to be level, but now I was reminded how the western side of the field ascended in a mild but persistent rise; and, to the northwest, how the unusual rock outcroppings offered climbing walls and geologic screens of privacy: a Paleolithic corner for the terrified caveman in all of us. Yes, I remembered now, here in the watchful safety of room 505, my eyes starting to tear up from the cleaning agents used by the orderlies or the thought of all the blood the doctors had stolen from my boy's delicate wrists, or maybe just from the vertigo of standing with him and seeing the Meadow again, that home and hellyard for all the lost children of my youth.

The city back then, infamously, teetered for several years on the cliff's edge of total bankruptcy. A chronic and mindblowing state of financial meltdown that by the early to middle seventies had infected to some degree most every institution in the five boroughs, municipal or private. A mosaic of urban decay into which the progressive private school on East Ninety-sixth Street attended by my older brother and me seemed to fit organically, a natural evolution: Located in a once-grand town house on the socioeconomic dividing line between the Upper East Side and Spanish Harlem, Manhattan Country School had never expected to have much money to spend anyway. The student body was small, there was no racial majority, and tuition was on a sliding scale based on income. More practically, unlike many other elementary schools nearby, ours didn't have its own athletic facilities but rented dodgeball and basketball time in the gym of the posh St. Bernard's School on Ninety-eighth Street. For all other recreational activities, weather permitting, Central Park was our playing field, free to all, to be shared with hundreds of other gymless kids, some of them from zip codes higher than we could count.

The park, for us, meant the Meadow, and the Meadow was our school away from school. I've never done the math, but it seems more than conceivable to me that between the ages of four and fourteen I spent a good 40 percent of my waking hours playing sports on that field and running reckless among those rocks. That some of the stuff I got up to continues to this day to bother and even haunt me is perhaps only right; as it ages, the city carries its rough earlier selves under its polished later guises, just as I do. History will record not only the misdemeanors and worse of yesteryear, but the banalities too: How, for instance, the Meadow's grass was all dead and rubbed away then, and we played our soccer and softball games in mud one day and in eye-stinging dust the next. How piles of dog shit were the rule, not the exception. How, during the tumble of play, shards of broken liquor bottles could turn your knees into little bloody legs of lamb. I'd heard of trees and shrubs cut down by the Parks Department because they'd sheltered rapists and muggers, and of a nightmarish water fountain that dribbled raw sewage into the mouths of toddlers. Whether or not such hearsay was true was beside the point; religion doesn't require proof. Nor does memory. The feeling of decline then was general over New York, is what I mean, and if you weren't careful enough, or tough enough, it could seep inside you and taint the way you saw the larger world (which wasn't doing too great itself). In any case, the only police I remember seeing around the Meadow were the two slow-moving, mustached patrol cops who took up virtually permanent residence next to the Sabrett hot dog guy in front of the Ninety-seventh Street entrance. A pair of dogs with everything and a soda went for a clean buck, though I still believe that the law then—being, like everything else in the city, bankrupt—ate its lunch for free.

I wouldn't want to give the misleading impression here that my brother and I lacked for anything material while we were growing up. On the contrary, our father was a successful attorney, and we lived in a large apartment on Ninety-fifth Street and Park Avenue; we were two of only a small number of students at our school whose parents paid full tuition. Of course, I see now that we were able to live in that apartment—which my parents had bought, amicably but at a bargain-bin price, from the parents of one of my brother's classmates—precisely because of the general economic climate. Boats were sinking everywhere but at different rates, which allowed the boats that were sinking more slowly (and having begun at higher tides of income) to now and again experience a queasy, fleeting mirage of moral uplift. That many of the marriages we knew, my parents' included, were rapidly deteriorating and would not survive the decade only added to the sense I had back then, that despite our relatively privileged economic position among our friends, the ground beneath my brother's and my feet was an unstable and ever-shifting surface; like the Meadow, mud one day and dust the next, and yet just enough of an outer fringe of grass, always, to suggest the stubborn, incongruous return of spring.

Compared to now, the streets of certain city neighborhoods in those days were shockingly unsafe. A teacher at Manhattan Country School—a wonderful man, much loved by all of us—was murdered in his Harlem apartment by a robber. I knew two kids who'd been "knifed." Over a span of seven or eight years my brother and I were mugged several times each (once a switchblade was waved close to me, another time I was punched in the face). Our father was mugged too, a knife held against his throat one mild evening, just two blocks from our apartment building. We were taught early and often that whatever you had in your pockets was "not worth your life"; you were to give it up without protest and move on. The real cost, of course, was the shame, which heavied your blood for weeks afterward, more than eclipsing whatever lightness the money or watch or bicycle had ever brought to your life before it was taken from you.

Shame—now there was a feeling which from an early age I intrinsically understood. For many years I was a short kid, and I mean very short, one of the three shortest in my class. (You see, I still remember how many of us there were.) And though I was a pretty good athlete and in my teens would eventually grow to a respectable height, and though in retrospect I'm grateful to having been small for adding to whatever sense of empathy I may have toward other people's infirmities, at the time I found my lack of physical stature in the world almost existentially confounding. My insufficiency was inside: not something valuable that had been stolen from me (as in a mugging, which I might've understood), but something priceless that had never been bestowed on me in the first place. An awareness, perhaps, which led to my developing the outwardly lively (and partially fake) personality that some people claim to have associated me with then, yet which, sadly, failed to elicit in me a commensurate sympathy for my vertically challenged brethren. I will never forget one winter afternoon in the Meadow when we were seven, stuffing a hard-packed ice-ball into the face of one of the other short boys in my class, who had never been anything but kind to me. I was taller than him by only half an inch, but that was enough for me to feel the need to dominate him and make him cry, which on that day I regretfully did.

The Meadow was our testing ground for such primitive urges, I now see, a kind of municipal Colosseum for midget gladiators. Within those largely unpoliced boundaries between 97th and 100th streets we could let loose our most basic instincts of fight and flight, wholly submit ourselves to the pain of each, and put away our thoughts of childish things.

It was in the Meadow that, one winter's day at the age of nine, I was mugged within sight of my class and teacher. It was not a dramatic event; it was just another day, really.

At that time it was not hyperbole to say that our school's entire stock of winter sports equipment consisted of two Flexible Flyer sleds, only one of which was operational.

During "park time" on days after a snowfall, our phys ed teacher—a large (in our eyes, giant), muscular, gravel-voiced ex-con of surpassing gentleness named Doc—would stack us two at a time on the lone steerable Flyer and, with huge hands, shove us down the mild hillock on the west side of the field (that slope which eventually I would forget existed). Each time the sled would be dragged back to the start line, we'd flock around it like baby penguins wanting food, crying out, "Doc! Doc! Doc!" If he picked you, I swear, you grew taller instantly. That particular day he grinned at me, and the other kids stepped aside. I lay down on that magical sled and took the steering bar in my gloved hands. Behind me I heard Doc call the name of one of the other short boys, and a moment later felt the boy's weight stretched along my back, pressing my ribs uncomfortably against the sled. A brief jostling between us for better position, our parkas rubbing with an insect whine; then a huge hand clamped down on us. Doc took three powerful strides, gave a shout of encouragement, and heaved us off.

The sled dropped over an invisible lip, rapidly gaining speed. What snow was left had melted and hardened overnight into a wide basin of rough gray ice that grew rougher and grayer as it thinned over the middle of the field. The metal runners scraped and whooshed beneath me. I heard a repetitive squeak and realized that the boy on my back was laughing. I began to laugh, too. We were both squeaking and laughing with the sled bumping over ruts and runnels in the ice, and then I heard a different sort of sound and felt a lightness and knew that somehow he'd tumbled off. I did not look back. I was on my own finally, across the middle of the field and still moving at a decent speed, approaching the two elm trees at the east boundary, beyond it nothing but the empty walking path and the exit. As far as I knew, no one from my school had ever made it this far on a Flexible Flyer sled; possibly it was a local record of some kind. The sweetness of my triumph began to dawn on me, and I let my feet drag over the ground, slowing my speed. Soon I'd stopped completely. For a while I just lay there, far from everyone, smiling to myself.

I didn't see them until they were almost on top of me. They'd been waiting for me behind the trees. Three teenagers. The tallest already had my sled in his hands. Frozen with fear, I did and said nothing. I watched them run with the sled out through the Ninety-ninth Street entrance and up Fifth Avenue.

Perhaps a minute later, Doc sprinted past me at full speed, following the boys out of the park.

I remained where I was, under the elms' naked branches.

Some minutes later, I saw Doc reenter the park. He was dragging the sled by its knotted pull-rope. He looked tired and unhappy with himself. Beside me he paused to touch my shoulder. "Not your fault," he said.

I have always wanted to believe him.

Doc did not tell me what, if anything, he'd done to those boys, and I did not ask.

Later that same year in the Meadow, in the company of three other classmates (a boy and two girls, not much of a gang), I discovered myself struggling to light a fire from a neat pile of dried twigs and leaves. It was the period before lunch. The four of us had secluded ourselves behind the highest of the rock outcroppings, and, using a matchbook stolen from the candy-and-cigar store around the corner from school, I tried again and again to produce a flame. My hand was shaking, and the green, early spring leaves weren't dry enough, and for a minute or two I was hopeful the kindling wouldn't catch. But then it did, and as an actual fire began to grow, my terror matched it exponentially, and, trying to reverse what I'd just done, I stamped my feet so near to the rising flames that their soles began to melt.

Later still in the Meadow, a few years later, a boy in my class called me out to fight. *The Meadow*, he hissed, *after school*. To me it sounded like a movie, not my life. But when, a little uncertain, I showed up in the Meadow after school, it turned out to be real. There he stood—taller, stronger—accompanied by another boy, some sort of second.

We faced off. I was scared, of course; but beyond that it was as though my heart had died inside me. The thought occurred to me that I should do something while the opportunity for action still existed. So I dove for his legs. My move caught him by surprise, and he fell backward. Pure instinct, I jumped on him and, for a fleeting moment, straddling his chest, cocked my fist back to punch him in the face.

There are two types of people who have no idea who they are, it seems to me. The first type feels emboldened to act because he has no idea who he is. The second type feels paralyzed to act because he has no idea who he is.

I remember the bigger boy on his back in the Meadow that day, staring up at me. It was only a moment, but long enough for me to permanently register his shock at finding himself in that exposed position; his expectation, almost a resignation, that he would soon get hit; and then the look of disgust on his face when he realized that I could not do it.

Some years after Doc left our school—he was let go, I believe, because of a couple of incidents of apparent drunkenness on the job—and after I was gone too (to a boarding school in Connecticut, a different world completely, though not necessarily a better one), a story went around about what had happened to him. According to the story, one morning a businessman stopping by a Citibank branch in the school's vicinity was alarmed to find a large unshaven black man curled on the floor, weeping behind his fists. The police were called, and they took the man away. It was Doc. He had entered the bank intending to rob it, but then he'd either lost or found his heart, and been unable to go through with his plan.

Last weekend, I took my son to the Meadow for the first time in his life. (We live in Brooklyn.) Call it an act of extreme nostalgia or perhaps a milquetoast exorcism. "This is where your uncle Matt and I used to play our sports," I told him as we approached the Ninety-ninth Street entrance on Fifth Avenue. It was a lovely day in midspring.

Above the exterior wall of the park there seemed to hang a chlorophyll radiance that I could not connect with the place I remembered. I tentatively filled my lungs with the anticipation of its greenness and did not tell my son about muggings or fires or how once, long ago, his daddy had been humiliated in a fight. We entered holding hands. Within a few feet we walked up to a high metal fence that circumscribed the entire Meadow, blocking our passage. On the fence was a sign. My son asked me what it said, and I read it to him: THE EAST MEADOW IS BEING RESTORED AND WILL REOPEN IN THE FALL. My son asked me what *restored* meant. I stood looking through the imposing fence past the two American elms to the lush, verdant lawn that stretched as far as I could see, and I told my son that it meant that the stories of our youth, no matter how far in the past or what beauties may have grown over them, are never completely finished.

BEN DOLNICK
Goodnight Moon

Y EARS AGO—WHEN I still thought that a writer was something that you could simply declare yourself to be, like a vegetarian—I took a summer job at the Central Park Zoo. At last, a subject!

I had, as I went about my life, been holding a series of unannounced auditions. Would college do as a setting for my first novel? No, I was still too shaken by the guidelines I'd once read for a short-story contest. (*However interesting you think your college life is, it isn't. No one cares.*) How about a corny, down-on-its-luck Italian restaurant like the one I grew up dragging my parents to in Maryland? Wouldn't that be fun, with the grumpy maître d' and the sulky, stoned waiters? Yes, but if I were able to trick a restaurant into hiring me, I would undoubtedly sever a fingertip in my first week. I considered a day-care center, a ski resort, a private detective's office. This seems now like an almost unfathomably stupid way to have gone about conceiving a first novel, but at the time it seemed to me an instance of admirable practicality. A handful of first novels that I admired—*Goodbye, Columbus*, *The Mysteries of Pittsburgh*—had been set during single summers, and what better way to occupy my narrator during his summer than with a summer job? (And, x-ing out multiple problems at once, what better way to occupy myself, in the time that I wasn't writing my novel, than by doing the very job that my novel would be about?)

So: the zoo.

I knew a thing or two about zoos, since my mom had designed exhibits for the National Zoo when I was growing up, and like any New Yorker I had a healthy love of Central Park. Had I ever been to the Central Park Zoo? I hadn't, but I went as soon as I sent in my application, so that I wouldn't have to lie during the interview. Did I plan on a career in zoos? Of course not, and I didn't even know enough to pretend otherwise. Had the zoo not been particularly short on keepers that summer, I would very likely not have gotten the job, and my first novel would have been a tale of romance and intrigue behind the scenes of a Verizon store or a Foot Locker. But they were short on keepers, and so the job was mine.

The Central Park Zoo, as I didn't really appreciate until I'd begun to work there, is small. And the Central Park Children's Zoo, which was where new hires tended to start, was considerably smaller, a minor city in a piddling state. As I entered the park each morning from its southeast

BEN DOLNICK

corner, passing between rows of benches on which nannies slumped behind overloaded strollers and caricaturists squinted before giggling tourists, I'd come after a few minutes to the main zoo on my left. I'd pass the stop-sign-shaped tank for the sea lions, who swam sleekly among their rocks. Farther back, various monkeys and penguins and even a polar bear or two. Any of these animals were, objectively speaking, more interesting than the ones I had been entrusted with, but by the end of my first week I gave them no more thought than I gave to the layers of rock underfoot. My zoo, my setting, was farther on.

I learned fairly quickly, in the kinds of conversations that people have while they shovel damp congealed layers of filthy hay into garbage bags, that our zoo was at the bottom of a well-recognized hierarchy. An ambitious keeper would move from the Children's Zoo to the main zoo and from the main zoo to Prospect Park and from Prospect Park to the Bronx. My co-keepers, many of them, *did* plan on having careers in zoos, and so they internalized this hierarchy in the same way that I, despite never having been published anywhere, knew just how much prestige accompanied publishing a story in this magazine or that one. These keepers leaped up when someone in the main zoo needed a replacement; they volunteered at park fund-raisers; they spent hours scraping hardened guinea fowl poop from concrete floors. They were, in other words, good employees. I was not.

Because what I'd discovered, and this was so obvious that I had a hard time articulating it even to myself, or admitting that I'd been surprised by it, was that if I was really

28

going to write about working at the zoo, I was first going to need to experience it. And experience does not alter its pace to suit your desire to be done with it already. Each eight-hour day, divided into periods of raking and sweeping, hosing and feeding, hauling and dumping, was like a plate of brussels sprouts that I was not allowed to leave the table until I'd finished. I had never had a purely physical job before, and I kept finding myself thinking, when I wasn't trying to remember the names of everyone I'd gone to elementary school with or the starting lineup of every championship team since the 1986 Celtics: *What are you supposed to do with your mind all day?*

I had envisioned, to the extent that I had bothered envisioning it at all, that working at the zoo, in addition to the inevitable drudgery, would consist of many redeemingly blissful hours in the company of animals. I was not naive enough, quite, to think that a chimpanzee and I would be strolling around the yard hand in hand, or that with a flick of my head I would have sea lions doing backflips, but I did imagine a vaguely cowboy-and-his-trusty-steed rapport developing between myself and my charges. I had loved many dogs in my life, and I didn't see why I shouldn't be able to feel something similar for these pigs and cows and sheep and goats, and why they shouldn't be able to feel something similar for me.

But in my first weeks I realized that these animals and I were destined to remain strangers in some basic sense. The pot-bellied pigs, Lily and Chili, never raised their heads to look at me. Lily snuffled around my boots, waiting to be fed, and Chili drowsed grumpily in his shed. (Chili turned out to be seriously sick, and he died at the vet one afternoon that July.) The birds and turtles cared no more for me than the rocks and branches did. The alpacas, Milo and Frankie, were actively hostile, perpetually in a state of idiotic alarm, preparing to spit. The sheep, of whom there were about a dozen, bashed each other with their ugly horns and demanded hay. The massive black bull, Othello, blundered around his pen like a sleepwalker having an angry dream.

My only solace, and it was a highly relative solace, was the goats. Another keeper had said to me, while he was showing me around, that they were as friendly as dogs, and this may almost have been true, if the dogs he had in mind were feral. The goats did consistently exhibit an awareness of humans' presences, and their interest in food pellets—the hard, brown, health cereal–looking bits that we both sold to the public and carried around ourselves—was so extreme that it was easy to mistake for affection for the people carrying them.

All but one of the goats were pygmies. These were small, about knee-height, and distinguishable at first mainly by their color. Spanky was black with a white patch on either side. (He looked as if he'd been spanked with hands dipped in white paint.) Pearl was all white, and her sister, Onyx, was all black. Their mother, Suzie, was salt-and-pepper. Each of them had a pair of gently curved, nicely grippable horns, which they would use a few times a day to get at an otherwise unscratchable place on their backs.

The lone non-pygmy, and the one animal whose existence gave me hope that the zoo might in fact be worth writing about, was named Newman. He was a Nubian goat, pure white, and about the size of a donkey with an extra-long neck. He had no horns and a pair of softly furred wattles hanging from his throat like jewelry. He wasn't fond of his keepers, but he was the one it was the least difficult to imagine being fond. When I would sit on one of the tree stumps that were scattered through the goats' pen like chairs in a waiting room, he would come over and poke his nose into my pockets in search of food. If he suspected that I was still holding out on him, he would begin to climb, on his knobby elbows, into my lap. Sometimes I scratched the place on his back that I was sure he would have scratched if he had horns, and he would reward me by baring his little teeth in pleasure. The campers who were our most frequent visitors loved him—he loomed over the other goats like a bobbing crane above a construction site—and so he got as much to eat as the rest of the goats combined.

Still, I can't quite account for why I felt so much warmer toward Newman than I did toward the rest of the animals. His silence may have had something to do with it (the rest of the goats were constantly belching/screaming), or it may just have been that, like Tom Hanks with his volleyball in *Cast Away*, I needed to make a friend of at least one of the nonhumans with whom I was for the time being stuck. Anyway, I began to write.

My first notion, and one that fizzled out before I'd written more than a few hundred words, was a bildungsroman in which Newman was the protagonist. A kind of magical realist fable in which he would go to school, live in an apartment, fall in love with a human woman, et cetera. In another draft I had him kidnapped from the zoo, only to turn up dead in the remains of a Santeria festival. (This version went nowhere in part because I feared it might earn me a visit from the Caribbean Anti-Defamation League.) In a third attempt, and the one that took the longest to reveal itself as foolish, I decided to have him popping up in a series of stories throughout the novel—in one as a rabbi, in another as a doctor, in a third as a stand-up comedian—like a kind of silent, four-legged Zelig, forever poking his head into the frame just as he poked his head into children's outstretched palms.

I think, in retrospect, that together these attempts amounted to a kind of pounding on a closed door. I would go back to my apartment at night and write scenes in which he died or escaped or sprouted wings, and then in the morning I would return to find him standing silent at the center of his pen, squinting in the sunlight. No bit of writing I did could get at him, except the bits I did that were about my not being able to get at him. He was a living rebuke, and not just to my notions of what I ought to write. I had self-pity like a lingering cold that summer—because of the rain and the tedium and the fact that a novel was proving as hard to write as everyone had said it would. And yet Newman, without a break room or a kitchen or the task of writing a book to distract him, seemed not to be suffering for an instant. Weekends meant nothing to him. Vacations and holidays didn't exist. There was no considering what to have for breakfast or where to go for dinner. Watching him—and I spent a great many hours that summer watching him—was like watching a monk meditating in a cave. How does he do it? What has he figured out? (Or maybe the better question, since suffering in conditions as mild as mine took some impressive contortions, was: What *hasn't* he figured out?)

The Buddha apparently taught a sermon that consisted entirely of his holding up a flower; the mere sight of it inspired, in at least a couple of onlookers, instant enlightenment. Newman didn't, of course, inspire anything nearly so dramatic as enlightenment in me, and I didn't have faith that I could do him sufficient justice to hold him up for anyone else. But if he was going to be in my novel (assuming, of course, that my novel was ever going to exist), I decided that it needed to be as something like that flower. A mute and irreducible demonstration. What are we supposed to do with our minds? What are we supposed to do with all these desires and these messy, aching, mortal bodies in which they're housed? How are we supposed to be happy? I had no more of an idea about any of this on the day, years later, when I finally finished my novel than I had on the day when I'd started it, but I did and do believe that Newman—whose picture I kept on my desk as long as I wrote—was as good an answer as any.

In the couple of years after the book came out, I tried to go back to visit him at least every few months. He didn't recognize me, of course, and he never stayed with me a minute longer than my food supply lasted. I imagined sometimes bringing him a copy of the novel, the cover of which featured a painting of his face, or at least telling him about it, but I knew that I might as well show off for a lamppost. He would, at best, have nibbled its pages before going off to find something tastier.

Still, I took great and strange comfort in knowing, as I passed the zoo on a walk across the park or even as I looked down on the city from a landing plane, that his life was carrying on more or less unchanged. While I got married and moved apartments and wrote another book, he stayed in his pen, his coat growing shaggier in winter and thinner in summer. During Hurricane Katrina, the Red Sox winning the pennant, the death of Michael Jackson, the financial crisis, the election of Barack Obama, and the invention of the iPad, he slept in his shed's warmest corner, ate food pellets when they were offered to anyone in his vicinity, and looked calmly at or past the people who stood watching him. I began to think of him as something like the moon, remote and miraculously constant.

A few weeks ago I realized that it had been a while since I'd taken one of these visits, at least a year, so on a freezing Sunday afternoon I took the train into Manhattan and told the heavily bundled man at the zoo-gate that I'd once worked there and wondered if I could go in and say hello. There were, on account of the cold, no visitors but me. The old food-pellet machines had been replaced, and dispensers of hand sanitizer had been mounted at various points.

I found Othello, the bull, facing the wall of his shed, as fearsome and gigantic as ever. Milo and Frankie darted brainlessly between the sheep.

I ought to have known, and maybe I did, as soon as I saw the new goats in the goat pen. They were something like the goats I'd known, but furry and brown, and one of them was a baby, as oddly proportioned as an infant in a Renaissance painting. While I stood watching them a keeper came out from the same back area where I'd spent dozens of afternoons hiding out from chores and rain, and I asked him about Newman, hoping he'd say that he'd been moved temporarily so that the new goats could get acclimated—or maybe that Newman, like my co-keepers that summer, had graduated to some other, more prestigious zoo. "He died about a year ago," the keeper told me. "Old age," he said. He'd become so skinny that you could see his ribs, and then all his hair had fallen out. He'd started to eat even more obsessively than usual, but he couldn't gain any weight. They put him to sleep in the same infirmary where we used to go pick up medicine for Chili and Lily.

We talked for a few minutes about the new goats—the baby was just seven weeks old—and the new pigs. The only one of the goats I'd known who was still alive was Suzie; her children, Onyx and Pearl, had died before her, and she, now loaded up on painkillers, had become so grumpy that they'd had to move her in with the sheep. There's nothing like the lives of animals, except possibly the lives of athletes, to make you appreciate the law of impermanence.

Walking back to the train, and then riding back to

Brooklyn, I had the feeling, as is not uncommon, that there was something smart I ought right then to have been thinking. I'd just learned that the moon, after all, had been put to sleep in a Central Park outbuilding. But I felt not much more than quietly sad, and I couldn't think of anything other than that I hoped they'd taken good care of him as he died, and given him peanut butter.

At home I pulled the picture of him back out of the closet where it had ended up in one or another office cleaning, and as I looked at it, over the next couple of days, I surprised myself by not thinking very much about the bits of our relationship that really had gone something like my horse-and-cowboy fantasies, when he would come lumbering over and open my palm with his snout or rest his head on my shoulder. Instead I found myself, like some oddly unsentimental friend, thinking about the equally many times—though I hadn't written about these, and so had for whole years at a time forgotten them—when he seemed to feel nothing at all for me. I would stand at the fence, calling his name, holding out hay, and if he did look over at me, it was only to huff and lie back down. At these times I'd felt like a kid who learns that the adult he most wants to play with is asleep or needs not to be bothered just now.

But now that he was dead, his majestic indifference seemed much more central to who he was than whatever bits of friendliness had allowed me to imagine that I actually knew him. Even Newman, whose every step and breath had taken place in sight of Fifth Avenue, whose every meal and defecation had been on public display, had retained an inner room into which he could retreat. The outer Newman, the one who looked into cameras with a half smile, was, as I kept learning and forgetting, an invention of whoever happened to be watching him. The inner one was—and would remain, whatever I thought or wrote—a mystery.

ADAM GOPNIK
Through the Children's Gate

WE CAME BACK to New York in 2000, after years away, to go through the Children's Gate, and make a home here for good. The Children's Gate exists, and you really can go through it. It's the name for the entrance to Central Park at Seventy-sixth Street and Fifth Avenue. The names of the gates—hardly more than openings in the low stone wall describing the park—are among its more poetic, less familiar monuments. In a moment of oddly Ruskinian whimsy, Frederick Law Olmsted and Calvert Vaux gave names to all the entrances of Central Park, calling them gates, each accommodating a class of person to enter there: a park for all the people with entrances for every kind. There was, and is, the Miners' Gate, and the Scholars' Gate, and—for a long time this was my favorite—the Strangers' Gate, high on the West Side. The Children's Gate is one of the lesser known, though the most inviting of all. On most days you can't even read its name, since a hot-dog-and-pretzel vendor parks his cart and his melancholy there twelve hours a day, right in front of where the stone is engraved. It's a shame, actually. For though it's been a long time since a miner walked through his gate, children really *do* come in and out of theirs all day and, being children, would love to know about it. Now my family had, in a way, decided to pass through as children, too.

This was true literally—we liked the playground and went there our first jet-lagged morning home—and metaphorically: We had decided to leave Paris for New York for the romance of childhood, for the good of the children. We wanted them to go not to baffling Parisian schools—where they would have gotten a terrific education, been cowed until seventeen, and only then begun to riot—but to a New York progressive school, where they'd get a terrific education and, we hoped, have a good time doing it. Childhood seemed too short to waste on preparation. And we wanted them to grow up in New York, to be natives here, as we could never be, to come in through the Children's Gate, not the Strangers' Gate.

A crowd came through the gate with us. Twenty-five years ago, Calvin Trillin could write of his nuclear family of two parents and two kids as being so strange a sight in New York that it was an attraction on bus tours, but by the time we came home, the city had been repopulated—some would say overrun—with children. It was now the drug addicts and transvestites and artists who were left muttering about the undesirable, short element taking over the neighborhood. New York had become, almost comically, a children's city again, with kiddie-coiffure joints where sex shops had once stood and bare, ruined singles bars turned into play-and-party centers. There was an excess of strollers so intense that notices forbidding them had to be posted at the entrances of certain restaurants, as previous generations of New Yorkers had warned people not to hitch their horses too close to the curb. There were even special matinees for babies—real babies, not just kids—where the wails of the small could be heard in the dark, in counterpoint to the dialogue of the great Meryl Streep dueting with a wet six-month-old. Whether you thought it was "suburbanized," "gentrified," or simply improved, that the city had altered was plain, and the children flooding its streets and parks and schools were the obvious sign.

The transformation of the city, and particularly the end of the constant shaping presence of violent crime, has been amazing, past all prediction, despite the facts that the transformation is not entirely complete and the new city is not entirely pleasing to everyone. Twenty some years ago, it was taken for granted that New York was hell, as Stanley Kauffmann wrote flatly in a review of Ralph Bakshi's now oddly forgotten New York cartoon-dystopia *Heavy Traffic*, and every movie showed it that way, with the steam rising from the manholes to gratify the nostrils of the psychos, as if all the infernal circles, one through thirty, inclusive, were right below. E. B. White was asked to update his famous essay about the city, and that unweepy man, barely able to clear the bitter tears from his prose, declined to write about a city he no longer knew. In the seventies, Robert Caro's life of Robert Moses, blankly subtitled "And the Fall of New York," was the standard version of What Had Happened.

Everyone has a moment of personal marvel about how far things have gone or changed: Twenty-three years ago, I recall, they were toting bodies out of the Film Center on Ninth Avenue, and (nice lost word) the degenerates were brooding on it at the Film Center Café. Now the Film Center shines and the café across the street serves mussels and croissant sandwiches, having kept its Art Moderne front, so "period," if nothing else. The scale of this miracle—and for anyone who remembers the mood of the city in the early seventies, miracle it is—leads inevitably to a rebound of complaint. It Is Not So Miraculous At All. Or: You call *that* a miracle? The cross-dressers in the Village sniff at the influx of nuclear families as the fleeing nuclear families once sniffed at the cross-dressers. Some of the complaining is offered in a tone of intelligent, disinterested urban commentary: The service and financial and media industries, they say, are too unstable a base for a big city to live and grow on (though, historically speaking, no one seems able to explain why these industries are any more perilous than the paper-box or ladies' lingerie industries of forgotten days).

Most of the beefs are aesthetic and offered in a tone of querulous nostalgia. What happened to all that ugliness, all that interesting despair, all that violence and seediness, the cabdrivers in their undershirts and the charming hookers in their heels? This is standard-issue human perversity. After they gentrify hell, the damned will complain that it was much more fun when everyone was running in circles: *Say what you will about the devil, at least he wasn't antiseptic. We didn't come to hell for the croissants.* But the lament has a subtler and more poignant side, too. All of us, right and left, make the new Times Square a butt of jokes—how sickening it still is to be forced to gaze at so much sleaze and human waste, to watch the sheer degradation of people forced to strut their wares in lust-inducing costumes before lip-licking onlookers, until at last *The Lion King* is over and you can flee the theater. These jokes are compulsive and irresistible because they speak to our embarrassment about our own relief, and to a certain disappointment, too. Safety and civic order are not sublime; these are awfully high rents to be paying to live, so to speak, in Minneapolis.

Still, croissants and crime are not lifestyle choices, to be taken according to taste; the reduction of fear, as anyone who has spent time in Harlem can attest, is a grace as large as any imaginable. To revise Chesterton slightly: People who refuse to be sentimental about the normal things don't end up being sentimental about nothing; they end up being sentimental about *anything*, shedding tears over old muggings and the perfect, glittering shards of the little crack vials, sparkling like diamonds in the gutter. *Où sont les neiges d'antan?*: Who cares if the snows were all of cocaine? We saw them falling and our hearts were glad.

The more serious argument is that the transformation is Parisian in the wrong way: the old bits of the city are taken over by the rich (or by yuppies, which somehow has a worse ring) while the poor and the unwashed are crowded right off the island. By a "city," after all, we mean more than an urban amusement park; we mean a collection of classes, trades, purposes, and functions that become a whole, giving us something more than rich people in their co-ops and condos staring at other rich people in their co-ops and condos. Those who make this argument see not a transformation but an ethnic cleansing, an expulsion of the wrong sort. Still, it is hard to compare the *Mad Max* blackout of '77 with the *Romper Room* blackout of '03 and insist that something has gone so terribly wrong with the city. No one can creditably infer a decline, which leads us back to the Times Square Disneyfication jokes. And toward remaking the old romance.

It is a strange thing to be the serpent in one's own garden, the snake in one's own grass. The suburbanization of New York is a fact, and a worrying one, and everyone has moments of real disappointment and distraction. The Soho where we came of age, with its organic intertwinings of art and food, commerce and cutting edge, is unrecognizable to us now—but then that Soho we knew was unrecognizable to its first émigrés, who by then had moved on to Tribeca. This is only to say that in the larger, inevitable human accounting of New York, there are gains and losses, a zero sum of urbanism: The great gain of civility and peace is offset by a loss of creative kinds of vitality and variety. (There are new horizons of Bohemia in Brooklyn and beyond, of course, but Brooklyn has its bards already, to sing its streets and smoke, as they will and do. My heart lies with the old island of small homes and big buildings, the sounds coming from one resonating against the sounding board of the other.)

But those losses are inevitably specific. There is always a new New York coming into being as the old one disappears. And that city—or cities; there are a lot of different ones on the same map—has its peculiar pleasures and absurdities as keen as any other's. The one I awakened to, and into— partly by intellectual affinity, and much more by the ringing of an alarm clock every morning at seven—was the civiliza- tion of childhood in New York. The phrase is owed to Iona Opie, the great scholar of children's games and rhymes, whom I got to interview once. "Childhood is a civilization with its own rules and rituals," she told me, charmingly but flatly, long before I had children of my own. "Children never refer to each other as children. They call themselves, rightly, people, and tell you what it is that people like them—their people—believe and do." The Children's Gate exists; you really can go through it.

MARK HELPRIN
Framed in Silver

A MONG HUNDREDS OF our family photographs in
cabinets, in boxes, and in albums or saved from them
as they come apart, a relative few have made it into silver
frames that stand in places of honor in the light. Some are
forty, fifty, a hundred years old or more, edited by history
at intervals of decades. The passage of time has clarified
what is important, and the telling expressions and attitudes
once hidden in the clutter and anxiety of the everyday have
lasted to burn through the years like a stream of molten
gold.

It is not so much the action or the location of these
portraits—and they are all portraits—that make them come
alive, but what is captured in the faces of the departed. The
photographer did not know and the camera could not
have known, but somehow the essence of the person knew
what was demanded and that it would have to speak

through time, with only a fraction of a second in which to jump into the future, to be still for eternity, and to outlast death. And as if by magic, it did.

There is my father as a young man in North Africa in the twenties, his black hair slicked back and full, his legs wrapped in puttees; and there he is twenty years later during the war, in uniform, surrounded by his military staff. There are he and my mother in the happiest year of their lives, on the beach at Amagansett, where they lived in a shack and my father fished and sold his catch at the Montauk docks. Looking out from behind the glass, they are sunburnt, young, and strong.

But of all the photographs in silver frames two stand out, placed near me now by accident and unconscious memory. Here is my mother by the window overlooking the park. You can tell by the light that it's afternoon. She is reading *The Great Gatsby*. It is the late forties, and she is roughly of the age that my daughters are now. Just coming off the peak of Broadway stardom, her career in the next decades will follow a steep, unrelieved, downward trajectory, ending with her in a wheelchair, afflicted, trying to mine comfort from yellowed newspaper clippings that now, long after her death, disintegrate when touched.

But in the photograph's patterns of light captured then and received now, she is extraordinarily beautiful. As an actress, she was changed by the presence of a camera, and her poses and assumed expressions were never fair to her. This is an exception. Perhaps she was happy that day, confident. Or perhaps for a moment she was able to see ahead.

She looks straight at the camera, unaffected, open, honest, her real self visible as a gift through time. She is as I had never seen or understood her. If only I could speak to her now, to tell her that at last I may know her.

The light that so beautifully illumines the left side of her face as she looks south eleven storeys above Central Park West comes in over the Reservoir and the tangle of leafless branches below. When my father returned from the war, he made a charcoal sketch of the park as seen from our windows, on Valentine's Day, 1945. It is buoyant and full of life because, only months before, being alive was a gift he thought he might have to do without. There is the northern pump house, the arched cast-iron-and-wood bridge, and though the gulls in a group over the Reservoir, as in a van Gogh, are messengers of mortality, they are small and distant, kept away and apart in great volumes of pale and roiling blue.

During my infancy no one ever bothered to tell me about the expanse of trees, fields, and lakes that I stared at over the window seat as I stood on tiptoe. I thought that what I saw was the entire world, that the immense line of buildings on Fifth Avenue, shadowed in morning, rose-colored in the setting sun, and sparkling in the dark, was Europe, where my father spent half the year at work. I believed that nature, although I didn't know its name, existed only in a huge rectangle set like a pool amidst a world of concrete and glass, and that the artificial world—which I thought was most of everything—orbited around it.

Such misapprehensions had lasting consequences. Before

the war, when the heat was insufferable, my parents would sometimes spend the night in the park. When much older, I was told that on such nights thousands of people would do this, as if they were neighbors in a small village. Late in the forties I myself was taken on a very hot night not to sleep but to walk through the park, and I saw there what I thought of as "big boys" swimming in the Reservoir. They would climb over the chain-link fence and swim to the north-south causeway, which most times is covered by a few inches of water and invisible. Later, when informed that Jesus could walk on water, I thought it was no big deal, as the Irish boys from Clinton did it all the time.

And if the park were sometimes packed sociably at night in the late forties, two decades on, primarily via late-night television, it had the reputation of being one of the most dangerous places in the world. Having just been graduated from college and soon to be a soldier, I decided to make a reconnaissance. So, on a summer night I went into the park at around two AM, when I thought it would be most dangerous. Breathing shallow breaths, I skulked along from tree to tree, scanning everywhere, trying to be silent. But I had the eight hundred acres all to myself. Soon I was so relaxed that I thought it would be completely safe just to lie down and sleep. But it wasn't quite warm enough for that, and, wanting to enjoy fully the extraordinary circumstance of being the only New Yorker in Central Park, I decided to sing.

After ten minutes' massacre of both parts of a duet from

West Side Story, "Only you . . . ," as I was walking down a paved path I nearly tripped over a cop who was sitting on a bench, his legs extended into the byway.

"Tell me you're not an actor, please," he said.

"I'm not."

"Good. You shouldn't be."

"Why is there no one here?" I asked.

"We're here."

"But no one else."

"There never is. Johnny Carson's an ass."

I was afraid that he might think I was a criminal. Given my duet, there was a chance. And perhaps because he was a cop, he knew what I was thinking.

"You're okay. There's no one to rob, so muggers don't come here. Squirrels are poor, kid. You've just discovered the safest place in the world, but don't tell anybody."

Not even ten years later, the park was more dangerous, perhaps because people had come back to it, which meant that in some minds it was once again rich in prey. Other than at night, it was most deserted in the midmorning after people had speed-walked through on their way to work. Often I would run around the Reservoir when no one else was there but Jacqueline Kennedy, after whom it is now named. Track is run counterclockwise so as to give the more powerful right leg its full potential when rounding turns, but at the Reservoir some officious someone made it the rule to run clockwise. I didn't abide by that, so several times a week I would pass Jacqueline Kennedy three times per circuit, which, as I remember, she usually made twice. She ran slowly, in a velour track suit that seemed to me to be much too heavy.

So, five or six times, we would approach, close, and pass. She always smiled graciously. Although she was the widow of the martyred president, she was alone, which led me to speed up when she was out of sight, to bring her back into view so I might keep watch over and protect her. And although she was famous throughout the world and had been the queen of what had been thought to have been Camelot, and I was just me, I was protective of her, and by her expression it was clear that though my vigilance may have been unnecessary she was appreciative and, I think, touched.

In more ways than one, I was completing a circle, for once very nearby someone had watched over me in a way I cannot ever forget, which brings me to the second picture, now closest to me and framed in silver. It has been on the mantle for years, near the clock, and the silver plate will no longer polish. I look at the photograph every day. More than sixty years old, though it was never exposed to the direct sun it is slowly disappearing—not fading, as photographs tend to do, but mysteriously darkening. I have watched this darkening for the more than a quarter of a century since my father died. The picture is a timepiece of sorts that seems not to move. And yet, it moves.

My father and I are in Central Park, on the path that leads from the playground at Ninety-third Street toward the Reservoir. I am about two. It is not long after the war, still the first half of the twentieth century. I know nothing of what has passed. You can see in his face that as someone who was born as the century turned, my father knows perhaps too much. I know nothing of what is to come. Having lived through the great wars and the small, he does. We are walking together, he in a double-breasted great coat, I in an absurd snowsuit. He has a Liberty of London scarf, and his hair is still as black as it was in the desert. I come up to his midthigh, a hood surrounds my face, and on top of it, and my head, is a pompom.

We have passed the playground that was the setting of my first dream, in which I flew from one outcropping of granite to another. Unknowing of the nature of dreams, when I awoke I believed that I had actually flown. I'm holding my father's hand, or, rather, he is holding mine, which disappears quite easily in his. Confident of his absolute protection, I think that as long as I am tethered and close, nothing can ever hurt me. He knows better.

What is he thinking? Perhaps he's thinking what I'm thinking now, that the paths are laden heavily, impossibly laden, with the traces of all those who have walked upon them. That this place, the park—a great square like no other, an eight-hundred-acre plaza around which hundreds of thousands live, some in high towers, some in tranquil brownstones, some in luxury, some in poverty—holds the record of innumerable lives and emotions and is the repository of memories that mount and remain, trapped by high, buff-colored walls that glitter when it is dark.

Although I dreamed that I could fly, I would not have dreamed that someday I would look back upon the invisible paths made by those whom I love and who are gone, that the picture in which I am walking in Central Park with my father would darken over time, like a clock about to mark the inevitable moment in which I will rejoin him. And then, perhaps as now I am aware of the invisible paths made by others, still others might feel, like the breeze you cannot see, the invisible paths made by me.

DAVID MICHAELIS
Carp in the Park

THIS WAS BEFORE earbuds, when our kids not only
heard us but believed we were telling the truth. One
night at the local Johnny Rockets, my then-wife and I
faced our children—two boys, ages nine and seven, and a
girl, four, all born in Washington, D.C.—and told them we
were moving: selling our house in Georgetown, buying
an apartment in New York City. We knew that it would be
hard, we said, but once we were settled, it was going to be
all right, because we would be living a half block from
Central Park. Someday we might move back home, but for
the time being the park was going to save us all.

Our older boy, Jamie, plunged straight out of the restaurant: gone from the table, sprinting up M Street. Clara
scooped up Henry and Diana and went in pursuit. I threw
down some money on our unfinished fries, glad to have
even a second to calculate how much we owed. My job in

those days was to make life normal again after something difficult, and I needed a moment to convince myself that once this crisis had passed, the children would resume their resilient ways. We had lived in that leafy, red-brick village along the slow Potomac for twelve years, and now that life was over.

I found my family a few minutes later outside the gold-domed Riggs Bank at M and Wisconsin, where Jamie had taken a firm stand in the parking lot. Flushed and defiant in the twilight air, his reddish hair aflame, he announced in great gulping gasps that he had money in this bank. He had earned it, he reminded us. He had sold lemonade and jars of honey with Benjamin and Gussie and Antonio and was going to stay right here and use that money to open an ice cream shop on Wisconsin Avenue. New York City was no part of the plan. He belonged here, not there; and to prove it, he said not another word but stood like a tree in the Riggs parking lot, eyes blazing.

We arrived three days after Labor Day, the family van plowing through the rush hour, the five of us sardined among fishing rods, summer junk, and an ailing Airedale whose twelve years had spanned the marriage.

At the far vanishing point of the elevated Bruckner roadway, the great city massed in silhouette, strangely noiseless under the open sky. The children stared out silently, taking it in against their will. The boys asked about graffiti, about getting mugged. Bright, blonde, four-year-old Diana, on the alert in the far backseat, piped up, as she had every hour for the last five: "Are we in New Wark yet?"

For weeks their mother and I had been running a shameless Clay Felker/Milton Glaser I ♥ NY campaign, guaranteeing VIP seats at Yankee Stadium, promising Wiggles concerts in Madison Square Garden, visits to the top of the Empire State Building, cool restaurants in Chinatown, actually watching the finish of the New York City Marathon . . . And sure enough, once we'd exited the Bruckner, crossed the Triborough, and squeezed onto FDR Drive, Jamie began making cheerful sounds about how he actually really liked what he saw. Henry, who had turned eight in July, remained wary. He was our nature boy, raised by wolves, relentless in pursuit of fish and game. We had had a big spring in Washington, he and I, fishing shad on the Potomac; and all through the summer, in New England waters, Henry had soothed himself through the initial prospects of the move by taking on catch-and-release fishing as his formal purpose in life.

Farther along the FDR, Henry's distrust finally turned to blank disbelief. When he saw the East River hurrying through its narrow, businesslike channel he wearily declared it to be awful: no place to fish, let alone to live. We would never catch anything here. Henry registered nothing when I told him about the Hudson, its tides, the leaping striped bass in the spring. Frustration mounting, eyes gone dead, he breathed the words ". . . *in the Potomac*," his throat thickening around something unutterable.

ĐĐĐĐĐĐ

Jamie reached in almost surgically and drew out the truth: "We'll never fish there again," he said, brother to brother.

Clara quickly broke in that of course we would, but Jamie's unprecedented authority had trumped our evasions.

We were not going back. Clara or I might have wished we could; one or the other of us might even think we were. The reality was that we were lying to ourselves. By opting for a geographic fix to a disintegrating marriage, by misleading the children "for their own good," we had exiled them from wide-sky childhood and marooned them in a big, scary, vertical city. It would be a hard time on this stone island. Whether or not Clara and I found a way to stick it out with each other, we were all shipwrecked here now.

Inside the van, it had fallen as quiet as a forest after a gunshot. For a few blocks it was not safe to say anything. The all-too-real New York City, busy with itself, indifferent to the latest newcomers, seemed to be building the children's case against us. I turned off Fifth and swung over to the West Side on the Eighty-sixth Street Transverse.

A few moments into the park, Henry broke the silence, mechanically inquiring, "Can we fish here?"

"Where?" I asked.

Honestly, there was nothing to see. Olmsted's sunken roadway had ducked us through a stone overpass, winding between retaining walls and past police stables, deliberately keeping us and the rest of the traffic out of sight as a greener, more promising upper world rose above us. Somewhere off to our right lapped the Reservoir, and I knew you couldn't fish there.

"*Where?*" I insisted.

I had lived on the Upper West Side during and after college—or, roughly, from the Wagnerian summer of the Son of Sam killings, by way of the rhapsodic opening of Woody Allen's *Manhattan*, to the bleaker era of the Central Park Jogger. Going fishing in that New York would have been a low stunt—a minor Philippe Petit statement against violence. Had you somehow blundered onto a fish, the general reaction would have been: *Yo! Ya caught a rat with fins! Ya not gonna to eat it, are ya?*

In the nineties, while I had gone to Washington and been starting a family, the park had been restored almost beyond imagination, and as we rolled up out of the transverse-road twilight into a startlingly enchanted Central Park West sunset, Henry brought Dutch sailor's eyes to the fresh green breast of this new park. Peering into the midst of the greatest experiment in metropolitan democracy, he said, "*There.* I want to fish there," and less than forty-eight hours later, we had our lines in the Lake.

It was a warm Saturday afternoon, guys rowing their dates around in the soupy, algae-thickened shallows off Hernshead, a little promontory in the Lake's western arm.

A part of me still couldn't believe that the waters of Central Park would teem with anything but condoms or crud. I felt like we were playing our parts in some *American*

Sportsman episode about angling the heart of Rudy Giuliani's post-9/11 New York, when, what do you know, my rod really was bending, and my heart pounding: sure enough, the Slug-Go had delivered, I was onto a nice fish—an eight- or nine-inch largemouth bass.

Jamie and I called out for Henry, but he was lost to the wild, having gone off by himself to fish from the boulders on the far side of the Hernshead outcrop. Besides, this was Jamie's day. For no sooner had I released my bass back into the Lake than he elatedly had one on his own line—his first fish of the summer, right here in New York, New York. He'd been skunked all July and August, while Henry had caught sixteen, donned his first waders, and developed an absurdly laid-back signature cast.

All business, Jamie cast back out into the Lake and straight off hooked a bluegill. By this time, the guys in the rowboats had caught on. They rested on their oars, challenging, maybe even willing, this most primitive male contest—man against fish—to show results to their dates, and when Jamie landed a third, they broke into a solid *Ghostbusters* round of applause, which he took in fully—a big, sweet, rusty-haired boy on the shore of the Lake, blushing, with a real fish struggling at the end of his line. No rat with fins here. Upon another round of cheers, he somehow knew to pump a fist and call out, "*Oh, yeah*"—and that, it seemed to me, was the moment he started to live in Manhattan. My Riggs Bank entrepreneur had found his customers.

Curiously, it was also the end of fishing in the park for Jamie. He never wanted to develop past the sweetness of those first triumphs. Of course, as the early, uncomfortable weeks at a new school unfolded, he could not get enough of it, and asked to go back to the Lake every morning and afternoon. That first Monday, the five of us had a picnic from Zabar's on the Great Lawn and afterward strolled over to the Lake to fulfill Jamie's wish for another magic fish moment. I remember this precisely because that was the evening when Diana, after her first day of pre-K at West Side Montessori, came up with "Daddy, did you know Charlie Parker plays bebop?"

"What!" I said. "How did you know that?"

"Sophie at my school has the sheet music."

A moon had risen over the boxy skyline of Central Park South. It was a gentle evening, the park shadowy and quiet, the air soft on one's skin. You could almost imagine that we had always lived here, knew what we were doing. That night, once again, Jamie caught and Henry didn't—two largemouth bass, both greeted again with applause, which itself was part of the wonder: *a fish in Central Park!* Fishing with two sons is tricky anywhere. Brothers are asymmetrical; one is always up when the other is down. But in the park, no matter which boy caught, or how many either one caught, or how big they got—and the boys got very big, of which more in a moment—people couldn't get over it, and neither could I.

The next June, after school was out for the summer, a shift came into our Central Park fishery one morning as Henry and I tried Hernshead before sunrise. Hooking up with a couple of bluegills in our usual spots, Henry got bored and picked his way back into a glade of overhanging trees and rock outcroppings, beneath which spread lagoon-like pools. I found him crouched on a tree limb and was horrified to see some large and unidentifiable presence threshing the shallows just below his perch.

Whatever might be in there, they were fierce and they were feeding—like baby alligators loose from the sewers. Delicately, we lowered Slug-Gos. But who were we kidding? We vowed to come back with the right lures.

"Did you see them underwater!" asked Henry. "Those weird orange glows," he mused. "What do you think they are?"

"Koi?" I said. "Monster catfish? Overgrown guppies?" My weird-meter was all over the place.

Next morning, after scattering bits of brown bread and baiting a hook, Henry hauled in a big fat carp—surely three pounds or better. Jamie had come along when he'd heard about the weird orange glows, and he also hooked up; but, keeping his line overtight, he let his beast get free and went home ahead of us, annoyed.

Meantime, back at the Mayor's Cup World-Class Carp Tournament, Henry netted a vast pale dildo out of the pond scum and wondered if this could be a condom. He was a month shy of nine. We had never discussed dildos, but I had recently done a brief Dad seminar on condoms, and so could reply, yeah, that's what it was, whereupon Henry observed, "That's a different kind of condom, Daddy." I said it sure was, and left it at that; though, good sort that I am, I slipped the thing into the Ziploc in which we'd brought an ear of sweet corn as carp bait, and tossed the whole package into a Conservancy trashcan, wondering what some nice park volunteer would think when he or she came upon a Ziploc containing one dildo and one corn cob.

Carp are big-bodied, with scales the texture of old rubber boots and soft tailfins tipped with that garish orange. Their vastly bloated minnow bodies are actually quite impressive—these dream fish, with imploring eyes—but something goes bad around their heads. The firm gold scales turn oily gray, and the face collapses into a gaping pink snout.

My gut reaction to catching these things? Severe nausea. At the same time I was very proud for Henry, when, that August, he fulfilled his stated goal of the spring, "I am going to catch a ten-pound carp, Daddy," with a fish so big that it became a marker in time. "You've had this rod since the Carp," I would still be telling him next spring. But I never ceased to be alarmed by the general size and shape and attitude of these freaks: on the one hand, their size and fleshiness and deliberation, on the other their strength and heaviness and angry struggle—as if we were hooking and unhooking barbs that had accidentally become embedded in the mouths of the boys' larger classmates.

This was partly because Henry had started bringing all his school chums to the Lake to go after carp; it had become the third-grade thing to do at Collegiate School that fall of 2006. And Henry got good at it. He could have run a guide service—tying on his own hooks, preparing all the rigs himself before coming out to the Lake, never missing a turn in the fisherman's knot I'd taught him in the now far-off summer of the move. His lines never snapped, and his carp were docile, almost obedient, like pets after a while—and always, huge. There would usually be a kid who had never fished anywhere before, let alone in Central Park; and always the rowboat guys with their dates, applauding now in total disbelief at the size of these mothers; and tourists, who were simply appalled. The Germans would ask quite seriously how we were going to eat them.

It took almost two full years before catch-and-release carp fishing became routine. By then, Clara and I were amicably divorced, the ailing Airedale had died, Diana was going on big-girl sleepovers with her jazzy friends, and the boys were now fly-fishermen, regularly testing flies. Henry and his friend Jack got good at taking carp on a streamer, or on bread, or both, landing them in a proper net. Through all the new scheduling between parents and apartments, we kept the gear organized; and the carp kept biting; you could always see them rising, those "weird orange glows." Henry, at school, got so wise to the folk humor of the city that one day he came home to announce happily that he had "played the Divorce card" on his history teacher, explaining to Mr. Chambers that he couldn't do his homework because his books were at his mother's and he "couldn't go there by court order."

Jamie turned out to be right. We never have fished the Potomac again. One of my memories of Henry's and my catching shad that spring before the move is of the worry that seized me whenever I had to unhook one of those silvery-bright fish. I could never catch my breath until the fish was returned to the river and things were back to normal. Only then would I know I hadn't harmed my son. I couldn't help it that spring: I felt sure that if I killed a fish during the unhooking, I would stamp Henry with its death forever. The carp in the park were, if anything, much worse at such moments. For one thing, there was always that audience; and then the enormous fish seemed so horribly helpless. But the real difference was that each time, with every prize catch that Henry and his friends released, as the fish got bigger and Henry grew more skilled at handling them, the fear of doing harm diminished, until last fall there came a day when Henry caught the biggest so far—a carp of something like twenty-four pounds, nearly halfway to the state record.

He was thirteen now, and I was remarried, living in a new apartment near the river, and it was no longer my place to step in. It took Henry a while to get the hook out. He worked with an intense, intimate calm, and the great fish thrashed against the rocks, blood trickling from its gills. Standing by, I imagined the worst. But my son took the gasping monster between confident hands, held the convulsed body firmly in the shallows until everything was all right, and let him go.

COLSON WHITEHEAD
The Colossus of New York

O N THE FIRST day of spring in search of antidote they seek the park, hardly aware of biological imperative. Everybody has the same idea. After all it's been a while. They've waited long months for this, have soldiered through slush and have worn sweaters. So it breaks in them with a snap, foot on twig: the Park. The one place they forgot to pave over. They'll get around to it someday. Be patient.

SHALL WE GO this way or that. Every day's essential either-orness made plain made paved in concrete: a forking path. Debate and deliberation until they sally arbitrarily. Just minutes in and the afternoon is set in stone. Whole possibilities canceled by this first mistake. People wear their first day of spring T-shirts, the true classics of their ragtag ensembles. Resentment fills the hearts of the regulars. Who are these savages. Every afternoon limping to this bench with her hoard of crusts. Her reach is audible as pigeons totter forward. Every evening walking the same path to the same tree, just to make sure it is still there. One solid thing in his life. Now these heathens with water bottles and look at that specimen sitting in my favorite spot.

WHERE TO SIT, where to sit. Our whole future depends on this choice. Strangers abound with their customs. A man and a woman pose on opposite benches, taking turns catching each other looking. Such extravagant speculations from so little. So goes the romance of the park bench. No one makes a move. Under the sun minutes expand until she gets up to leave. Wouldn't work out anyway. Shriveled men have determined that the average time spent on a park bench is seventeen minutes. Your tax dollars at work. In their green vehicles the deputies of the Parks Department keep the peace. They know the best spots to get a little shut-eye when their bosses go out for lunch. Keep off the grass. This section closed. Scheduled to reopen three weeks ago yesterday. One girl uses chalk to sketch a hopscotch board, another the Virgin Mary. The rain will wash it all away from agnostic cement. Some ducks. He's definitely wearing the wrong shoes. Smile, everybody, smile.

WATCH OUT for horses and wake manure. Watch out for humans on conveyances. Trusted servants heave wheel-chaired heiresses. Rollerblading yuppies burn off brunch.

Always some jerk on a unicycle. A yogi demonstrates his amazing powers and mimes on their day off expound endlessly. In the air softballs shuttle, Frisbees wobble and epithets hurtle. Some things are more easily caught than others. This gang on skates explodes from the left and right of him and fly from him like sparks. So you lie. Flat on your back on the grass. Such a rich blue. What are you thinking about. Nothing. She calls this rise Heartbreak Hill because that's what it is. For three years out of key with his time he studied the ancient martial arts in order to stand here looking stupid practicing in public. Dead men dynamited rock to undo glacial handiwork but holdout boulders remain, unwilling to part with deeds. Climbing across them children find themselves on the moon. This is genuine Manhattan schist. Accept no substitutes. In search of bygone days he wanders. The tree he and his brother used to climb is no longer so tall, and kids since have snapped off the branches they made rungs. He climbs up anyway. Thirteen stitches.

IT'S A little-known fact that people are buried here but only the murderers know the exact locations. Invisible wet stuff on the ground and here's a dead squirrel. So much for the picnic. Cross-legged summits. Welcome to the Riviera. Mistakes have been made in the area of shorts. This guy's nuts hang out as he sits Indian-style and she should really consider waxing if she's going to leave the house like that. Bushes, hedges, dark thickets. Don't go too far, kids, there are areas used for anonymous sex. Let's have anonymous sex, what do you say. Don't touch it, you'll get rabies. Prod it with a stick instead.

THE FAMOUS photographer prowls here for real-life stuff with his camera as victims enact. Years from now she will see her photograph in a gallery and wonder why she was crying. He touches her arm and says, I just want to make you happy. Oh. Some kids recently fucked in this spot under the eyes of those in the penthouse apartments. Inevitable spike in binocular sales this time of year. The giant digital clock above the corporate headquarters warns them of curfew. He says, See that window, pointing. No, that one. That's where I used to live. The new occupants gloat and glower behind tinted glass. Paperbacks bend on spines. Dogs hike legs. Some of the less talented hippies do a jig.

EMPIRE OF BROKEN teeth, scraped knees and tiny bits of glass. He is the king of the playground thanks to his hormonal problem, stealing toys and cutting line at the slide. His mother pretends not to notice and consults the article in her purse about that new medication. Intrigue by the jungle gym: the twins in striped shirts plan a coup. Parents gossip on benches. See, it runs in the family. Rumor has it this is where she met her new husband; their kids got into a fight in the tree house and they looked into each other's eyes and just knew. Where's her bottle. What's that sound. The swing set squeaks, a gargoyle tuning instruments. Mayo gone translucent in the heat. Under low stone bridges trolls are invisible. He thought this path was the way out but instead it takes him farther in. Then the spectacular malevolence of a cloud. You can see it creeping across the meadow before it hits you. So cold and abrupt. Like a friend.

SO MANY PEOPLE running. Is something chasing them. Yes, something different is chasing each of them and gaining slowly. She feels fit and trim. People remove layers one by one the deeper they get into the park. The sweaters keep falling from their waists no matter how they tie them. The matching strides of the jogging pair give no indication that after she tells her secret he will stop and bend and put his palms to his knees. Like some of the trees here, some of today's miseries are evergreen. Others merely deciduous. This is his tenth attempt to join the jogging culture. This latest outfit will do the trick. Pant and heave. How much farther. Reservoir of what. Small devices keep track of ingrown miles. Unfold these laps from their tight circuit to make marathons. It's his best time yet, never to be repeated. If he had known, he would have saved it for after a hard day at the office or a marital argument. Instead all he has is sweat stains to commemorate. One convert says, I'm going to come here every day from now on. It's so refreshing.

WHAT WE REALLY need are popsicles. If they'd foreseen this heat, the vendors would have stocked up on ice. Lukewarm lemonade but who can complain. Let's move to the shade. Fools wade in fountains. Their family looks happier than yours. This is where they came on their first date, so he steers her to this grove and hopes she will realize the error of her ways. She looks at her watch. Sunlight catches on glass surfaces and bits of metal. Glad we came but now I'm tired. It's not really a shortcut, cutting across the park, because there are places he cannot walk, that are fenced off, there are no direct paths and there goes his chance of making the surprise party. Behind that rock they smoke a joint. Next time less spit, please. For an assignment for school he collects leaves and twigs for examination under microscope. Bear away bits and pieces of this place. You probably need a permit.

IT'S GOT BIRDS and a steady ratio of human-to-guano contact. It's got weeping willows. They remind me of me. It has ponds. People can't see themselves and pronounce ponds murky but in fact they are perfect mirrors. Great day to be a caricaturist—everyone remembered to bring their faces. Benign sketches will be forgotten under benches and bus seats. The more damning ones lead to new haircuts. Is my nose really that big. Skin obscured all winter is out of practice. Have I always had this mole and if so is it getting bigger. His conspicuous long sleeves hide hesitation marks, souvenirs of that bad summer. The lines at the fountain are too long. Superpowerful nozzles drench faces. He runs along, shouting encouragement to his kite. Great day for flying a kite. Tried it in the middle of Broadway once, what a disaster. The boy starts spinning around and around in order to get dizzy and look at his funny walk. Pull up your drawers, girl. He says, I wish we had kids, blaming her with his tone. He never comes here even though he only lives two blocks away and now that he has forced himself to take in the sunshine everything is still terrible. Isn't that the cutest puppy. The old philosophers said it best: picking up chicks at the dog run is easy. No particular place to be. Just taking it all in.

GREEN. For whole minutes it is as if you live somewhere else than where you do. And what is that like. Like there are other choices. And then one bullying highrise pokes its head up west, then another, and a whole gang of them east and suddenly come out with your hands up, you're surrounded. Regiments on all sides. Armies don't get better than this. Stray too close to the edge and you'll be reminded as edifices frown down. Not yet. She goes deeper in.

THE BENCH she chooses turns out to be the location of the dance performance. Dancers and musicians hang a shingle in a good-luck spot according to their subculture. Just her and them at first but then the drums summon strollers, one couple, then ten, soon swaying human rings. Latecomers want to know what's going on in there. I'm always too late. People can't help themselves and feet tap, fingers tap. After untold basement rehearsals the dancers have it down pat. Look around. Brought together in this moment in a park on the first day of spring. A community. And fancy that in a city. Back to a time before zoning and rebar, one tribe, drums talking. Something that cannot be planned. Everybody knows they must remember this feeling because soon it is back to the usual debasement, and they try to remember and then it stops. Cash and coins fill the small basket. Cheapskates avert their eyes and then everybody moves on to that next brief oasis. It never happened. Except her on that bench. She stretches her arms. What a nice day.

ALL AT ONCE they want to go home. Something about the light. Everyone knows how to fold a blanket. Responsible citizens clean up, retrieving bits of themselves from blades of grass. Anything you brought here you must take away. Anything you found here must remain: it can't exist outside. People hear traffic as they get close to traffic and remember rules. Big hungry city but some relief: they know the rules again. At the Don't Walk sign he comes to his senses, possessing dinner plans. He sighs. Glad that's over.

FRANCINE PROSE
Some Music in the Park

WHEN I WAS growing up in Brooklyn, we had a front and back yard. It would never have occurred to us to go to Central Park in order to immerse ourselves in nature. Two postage stamps of meticulously mown lawn, a few trees, some tidy hydrangea bushes, a stand of daffodils that magically reappeared every spring—why would a person have wanted any more nature than that? And why would I have needed Central Park Lake when we had our own plastic wading pool decorated with grinning fish and ducklings in sailor hats?

On those rare occasions when an actual park was required—to sled down a hill, to visit a zoo, to ride on a carousel—we Brooklynites had Prospect Park and the Brooklyn Botanic Garden to supply everything we might want in the way of a snowy incline, a monkey house, or a merry-go-round. We even had our own cherry blossoms!

If, once a year or so, my family experienced a yearning for exotica, we could drive to the exotic Bronx to see the lions and tigers in its far more serious zoo.

And so throughout my childhood and most of my adolescence, Central Park was, so to speak, terra incognita. Until my last years of high school and the college summers (this was in the late sixties) when I discovered Central Park as a place where, counterintuitively, one went not for nature but rather for culture.

None of my friends and I liked the summer jobs we had (the summer after freshman year, I failed miserably as a file clerk), but we did like meeting up after work and going to Central Park to hear music or watch a play. How grown-up we felt, unrolling the blanket that someone had brought and unpacking someone else's mom-made picnic supper and drinking wine from a bottle in a paper bag as we waited to hear Tchaikovky's *1812 Overture*, which the New York Philharmonic played every year sometime around the Fourth of July. How sophisticated it made us feel, knowing that the overture's opening bars had been appropriated by Ike Turner for an Ike and Tina Turner song. And how quickly that sophistication vanished when fireworks erupted over the overture's closing bars and we heard ourselves squealing like children at a fireworks display.

It was not yet the trial-by-waiting-in-line that it would later become to pick up tickets for the Joe Papp productions of Shakespeare in the park; you could show up around dinnertime and get in. Many of those performances became the subject of legend, the masterpiece in which this or that future theatrical genius played the career-changing role. I very well may have seen George C. Scott and James Earl Jones in *The Merchant of Venice*, or Raul Julia as Othello, or Meryl Streep as Kate in *The Taming of the Shrew*. But the truth is, I can't remember.

Once I read that song lyrics are stored in a particular part of the brain. Perhaps the same is true of music in general, because the Central Park performances I remember most clearly were concerts, two concerts, thirty years apart.

The first was a Nina Simone concert in the summer of 1966. In her memoir, *I Put a Spell on You*, Simone recalls that the concert took place on the same night the Reverend Martin Luther King Jr. was stabbed in Chicago. In fact, on August 4, 1966, Dr. King was hit by a rock during a demonstration for fair housing in Chicago. For all I know, that was the night of the concert. In any case, that was the political climate; the subject of civil rights was very much in the air. It was a summer of racial confrontations: tense, explosive, violent. Less than two years later, Dr. King would be shot.

What I remember is Nina Simone giving the performance of someone who had been told, just as she was going on stage, that the Reverend Martin Luther King Jr. had that day been stabbed—or struck by a rock—in Chicago.

My heart goes out to the boy with whom I went to the concert. We were on a date. After my failure at being a file clerk the previous year, I'd decided to take some summer courses at Columbia. For some reason, one of them was an introductory studio architecture class, a peculiar choice for a person like myself who has never been able to think in three dimensions. The boy, a fellow student, had invited me to the Central Park concert after having spent much of the summer gathering the nerve to ask me out.

Surely, he had imagined something different from what we saw on stage. Perhaps he didn't know very much about Nina Simone. Surely he couldn't have predicted the unfortunate concurrence of the concert and the attack on Dr. King. Doubtless he had something more romantic in mind, or anyway something more neutral, something more like Sarah Vaughan singing jazz ballads.

There was nothing neutral about Nina Simone's performance. She sang "Strange Fruit," which is about the bodies of lynching victims hanging from trees in the South. She sang "Four Women," which is about the oppression—slavery, rape, prostitution—of African American women. She sang "Mississippi Goddam," a song inspired by the murder of Medgar Evers and the church bombing in Birmingham, Alabama, that killed four little girls. Every time she said *Goddam*, she spit the word at the audience. I had never seen a performer, let alone a woman, let alone a black woman, be that angry on stage. She was telling us that, to paraphrase a saying popular in those days, we were not part of the solution; we were part of the problem.

To say that the Nina Simone concert was life-changing would be an understatement. It expanded forever my sense of what could be done in art—the range, the power, the intensity, the freedom. It confirmed my sense (which had been growing all summer) that I definitely did not want to be an architect.

The concert was not, by any stretch of the imagination, romantic. By the time Nina Simone sang "I Loves You, Porgy," it was way too late to bring up the subject of love. After that evening, the boy and I were polite and distant in class, and we were both relieved when the course ended, a week or so later.

The second concert, in September 1997, was also astonishing, though in a very different way. This time the performers were Chaka Khan and James Brown. This time I went with my son Leon, who was a sophomore in high school—and a serious James Brown fan.

What I remember most clearly is that Leon had the flu and was running a fever of 102 and that I kept anxiously feeling his forehead as we made our way through the crowds of people (where had they all come from?) rollerblading, jogging, and sunbathing on the brilliant Indian-summer Sunday afternoon. No matter how I'd tried to convince him that he was too ill to go, he refused to miss the chance to see his idol.

Chaka Khan opened for the Godfather of Soul, whose arrival onstage was preceded by a fifteen-piece orchestra. The concert also included a cameo appearance by the Reverend Al Sharpton, who at one time had been James Brown's road manager.

I had seen James Brown perform several times before; in fact I'd been at the legendary 1968 Boston Garden concert at which he'd more or less single-handedly (with the help of the Famous Flames and his dancers, the Baby Jewels) quashed the riot simmering in the immediate wake of Martin Luther King's assassination. But though, at sixty-four,

James Brown was no longer doing the dramatic splits that had been his trademark, he still put on an extraordinary show.

Dressed in a red sequined suit, Brown was surrounded by a horn section dressed entirely in white and doing elaborately choreographed moves, and by dancers and backup singers, some of whom—in accordance with the event's vaguely patriotic theme—wore red-white-and-blue outfits that featured spangled hot pants. He sang "Gonna Have a Funky Good Time" and a bit of "Try Me" and of course "Please Please Please," falling to the stage until he had to be led off to the wings, only to break loose from his comforters and return for another chorus of begging and pleading his lover (or the audience) not to go as the MC gently placed an outrageously garish red cape around his shoulders. When he sang "It's a Man's Man's Man's World," a song I've always detested, he almost had me convinced that the male-created and male-dominated universe "wouldn't be nothing without a woman or a girl." And when he did a long rendition of "Sex Machine" as a finale, I recaptured that feeling I recalled from seeing James Brown when I was younger and he was in his prime: that visceral sensation that starts at the base of your throat and makes you want to make a sound like . . . well, like a kid watching fireworks.

My son was transfixed throughout, and neither of us minded the fact that we were standing all during the show. In fact, each time I felt Leon's forehead, it seemed to me that he was getting less feverish with every song. James Brown used to say that his aim in performing was to give people more than whatever they came for, and certainly that was true in our case: not only great music and entertainment, but in addition, a healing—a semi-miraculous near-recovery from an unpleasant flu.

As we left the dusty ground of SummerStage, the afternoon light appeared to have grown even more golden and burnished. All around us, New Yorkers were taking a Sunday break from the hustle and pressure of urban life, and as I walked among them, I felt grateful for having been given yet another transformative encounter with great music, and a great artist, in the heart of the city, in the midst of Central Park.

JONATHAN SAFRAN FOER
The Sixth Borough

O NCE UPON A time, New York City had a Sixth Borough. You won't read about it in any of the history books, because there's nothing—save for the circumstantial evidence in Central Park—to prove that it was there at all. Which makes its existence very easy to dismiss. Especially in a time like this one, when the world is so unpredictable, and it takes all of one's resources just to get by in the present tense. But even though most people will say they have no time or reason to believe in the Sixth Borough, and don't believe in the Sixth Borough, they will still use the word "believe."

The Sixth Borough was an island, separated from Manhattan by a thin body of water, whose narrowest crossing happened to equal the world's long jump record, such that exactly one person on earth could go from Manhattan to the Sixth Borough without getting wet. A huge party was made of the yearly leap. Bagels were strung from island to island on special spaghetti, samosas were bowled at baguettes, Greek salads were thrown like confetti. The children of New York captured fireflies in glass jars, which they floated between the boroughs. The bugs would slowly asphyxiate, flickering rapidly for their last few minutes of life. If it was timed right, the river shimmered as the jumper crossed it.

When the time finally came, the long jumper would run the entire width of Manhattan. New Yorkers rooted him on from opposite sides of the street, from the windows of their apartments and offices, from the branches of the trees. And when he leapt, New Yorkers cheered from the banks of both Manhattan and the Sixth Borough, cheering on the jumper, and cheering on each other. For those few moments that the jumper was in the air, every New Yorker felt capable of flight.

Or perhaps "suspension" is a better word. Because what was so inspiring about the leap was not how the jumper got from one borough to the other, but how he stayed between them for so long.

One year—many, many years ago—the end of the jumper's big toe touched the surface of the water and caused a little ripple. People gasped, as the ripple traveled out from the Sixth Borough back toward Manhattan, knocking the jars of fireflies against one another like wind chimes.

"You must have gotten a bad start!" a Manhattan councilman hollered from across the water.

The jumper nodded no, more confused than ashamed.

"You had the wind in your face," a Sixth Borough councilman suggested, offering a towel for the jumper's foot.

The jumper shook his head.

"Perhaps he ate too much for lunch," said one onlooker to another.

"Or maybe he's past his prime," said another, who'd brought his kids to watch the leap.

"I bet his heart wasn't in it," said another. "You just can't expect to jump that far without some serious feeling."

"No," the jumper said to all of the speculation. "None of that's right. I jumped just fine."

The revelation traveled across the onlookers like the ripple caused by the toe, and when the mayor of New York City spoke it aloud, everyone sighed in agreement: "The Sixth Borough is moving."

Each year after, a few inches at a time, the Sixth Borough receded from New York. One year, the long jumper's entire foot got wet, and after a number of years, his shin, and after many, many years—so many years that no one could even remember what it was like to celebrate without anxiety—the jumper had to reach out his arms and grab at the Sixth Borough fully extended, and then, sadly, he couldn't touch it at all. The eight bridges between Manhattan and the Sixth Borough strained and finally crumbled, one at a time, into the water. The tunnels were pulled too thin to hold anything at all.

The phone and electrical lines snapped, requiring Sixth Boroughers to revert to old-fashioned technologies, most of which resembled children's toys: they used magnifying glasses to reheat their carry-out; they folded important documents into paper airplanes and threw them from one office building window into another; those fireflies in glass jars, which had once been used merely for decorative purposes during the festivals of the leap, were now found in every room of every apartment, taking the place of artificial light.

The very same engineers who dealt with the Leaning Tower of Pisa were brought over to assess the situation.

"It wants to go," they said.

"Well, what can you say about that?" the mayor of New York asked.

To which they replied, "There's nothing to say about that."

Of course they tried to save it. Although "save" might not be the right word, as it did seem to want to go. Maybe "detain" is the right word. Chains were moored to the banks of the islands, but the links soon snapped. Concrete pilings were poured around the perimeter of the Sixth Borough, but they, too, failed. Harnesses failed, magnets failed, even prayer failed.

Young friends, whose string-and-tin-can phone extended from island to island, had to pay out more and more string, as if letting kites go higher and higher.

"It's getting almost impossible to hear you," said the young girl from her bedroom in Manhattan, as she squinted through a pair of her father's binoculars, trying to find her friend's window.

"I'll holler if I have to," said her friend from his bedroom in the Sixth Borough, aiming last birthday's telescope at her apartment.

The string between them grew incredibly long, so long it had to be extended with many other strings tied together: the wind of his yo-yo, the pull from her talking doll, the twine that had fastened his father's diary, the waxy string that had kept her grandmother's pearls around her neck and off the floor, the thread that had separated his great-uncle's childhood quilt from a pile of rags. Contained within everything they shared with one another were the yo-yo, the doll, the diary, the necklace, and the quilt. They had more and more to tell each other, and less and less string.

The boy asked the girl to say "I love you" into her can, giving her no further explanation.

And she didn't ask for any, or say, "That's silly" or "We're too young for love" or even suggest that she was saying "I love you" because he asked her to. Her words traveled the yo-yo, the doll, the diary, the necklace, the quilt, the clothes-line, the birthday present, the harp, the tea bag, the table lamp, the tennis racket, the hem of the skirt he one day should have pulled from her body. The boy covered his can with a lid, removed it from the string, and put her love from him on a shelf in his closet. Of course, he could never open the can, because then he would lose its contents. It was enough just to know that it was there.

Some, like that boy's family, wouldn't leave the Sixth Borough. Some said: "Why should we? It's the rest of the world that's moving. Our borough is fixed. Let them leave

Manhattan." How can you prove someone like that wrong? And who would want to?

For most Sixth Boroughers, though, there was no question of refusing to accept the obvious, just as there was no underlying stubbornness, or principle, or bravery. They just didn't want to go. They liked their lives and didn't want to change. So they floated away, one inch at a time.

All of which brings us to Central Park.

Central Park didn't used to be where it now is. It used to rest squarely in the center of the Sixth Borough; it was the joy of the borough, its heart. But once it was clear that the Sixth Borough was receding for good, that it couldn't be saved or detained, it was decided, by New York City referendum, to salvage the park. (The vote was unanimous. Even the most obdurate Sixth Boroughers acknowledged what must be done.) Enormous hooks were driven deep into ground, and the park was pulled, by the people of New York, like a rug across a floor, from the Sixth Borough into Manhattan.

Children were allowed to lie down on the park as it was being moved. This was considered a concession, although no one knew why a concession was necessary, or why it was to children that this concession must be made. The biggest fireworks show in history lighted the skies of New York City that night, and the Philharmonic played its heart out.

The children of New York lay on their backs, body to body, filling every inch of the park as if it had been designed for them and that moment. The fireworks sprinkled down, dissolving in the air just before they reached the ground, and the children were pulled, one inch and one second at a time, into Manhattan and adulthood. By the time the park found its current resting place, every single one of the children had fallen asleep, and the park was a mosaic of their dreams. Some hollered out, some smiled unconsciously, some were perfectly still.

Was there really a Sixth Borough?

There's no irrefutable evidence.

There's nothing that could convince someone who doesn't want to be convinced.

But there is an abundance of clues that would give the wanting believer something to hold on to: in the peculiar fossil record of Central Park, in the incongruous pH level of the reservoir, in the placement of certain tanks at the zoo (which correspond to the holes left by the gigantic hooks that pulled the park from borough to borough).

There is a tree—just 24 paces due east from the entrance to the merry-go-round—into whose trunk are carved two names. They don't appear in any phone book or census. They are absent from all hospital and tax and voting records. There is no evidence whatsoever of their existence, other than the proclamation on the tree.

Here's a fact: no less than 5 percent of the names carved into the trees of Central Park are of unknown origin.

As all of the Sixth Borough's documents floated away with the Sixth Borough, we will never be able to prove that those names belonged to residents of the Sixth Borough, and were carved when Central Park still resided there, instead of in Manhattan. So some believe that they are made-up names and, to take the doubt a step further, that the gestures of love were made-up gestures. Others believe other things.

But it's hard for anyone, even the most cynical of cynics, to spend more than a few minutes in Central Park without feeling that he or she is experiencing some tense in addition to just the present. Maybe it's our own nostalgia for what's past, or our own hopes for what's to come. Or maybe it's the residue of the dreams from that night the park was moved, when all of the children of New York City exercised their subconsciouses at once. Maybe we miss what they had lost, and yearn for what they wanted.

There's a gigantic hole in the middle of the Sixth Borough where Central Park used to be. As the island moves across the planet, it acts like a frame, displaying what lies beneath it.

The Sixth Borough is now in Antarctica. The sidewalks are covered in ice, the stained glass of the public library is straining under the weight of the snow. There are frozen fountains in frozen neighborhood parks, where frozen children are frozen at the peaks of their swings—the frozen ropes holding them in flight. The tzitzit of frozen little Jewish boys are frozen, as are the strands of their frozen mothers' frozen wigs. Livery horses are frozen mid-trot, flea-market vendors are frozen mid-haggle, middle-aged women are frozen in the middle of their lives. The gavels of frozen judges are frozen between guilty and innocent.

On the ground are the crystals of the frozen first breaths of babies, and those of the last gasps of the dying. On a frozen shelf, in a closet frozen shut, is a can with a voice inside it.

NATHANIEL RICH

Squawkeye and Gang on the Dendur Plateau

B Y FAR THE worst place to play football in Central
Park is the raised field at Eighty-fourth Street and Fifth
Avenue, adjacent to the Metropolitan Museum. The field
runs east to west. On each of its four sides there are hazards
that present ample opportunities for violent injury and
death. The least dangerous boundary is the west end zone,
which is marked by a slight attenuation of the field, in which
there stand two trees with thick, spread branches—excellent
for dashing in your brains when you're sprinting at full
speed to catch a Hail Mary. The east end zone is much
worse. It terminates at a short, chest-high fence. Beyond
this there is a thirty-foot drop onto a concrete ramp.

At the northern sideline the field slopes down in a declivity
so steep that, once breached, it is impossible to reverse
course. The force of gravity leaves you with two options: gallop, frantically, praying to avoid an ankle sprain, all the way

down; or stumble and roll, head over foot, all the way down. Along the entire southern side of the field is the Met's Temple of Dendur gallery. That sideline is a clear wall of glass.

The field itself, by the way, is crap. That isn't a euphemism. Apparently the Dendur plateau is one of the best places to walk your dog on the Upper East Side. The dog owners can get away with not cleaning up after their animals because the field, for most of the year, is dirt or even mud, so the feces blends in. Grass never seems to grow very well there. I don't know why. It might be due to the fact that the field lies on a hill, above a parking garage. Or maybe it's because of all the dog shit.

Nevertheless, this field is a sacred place for me, and not because it's next to a holy shrine to Osiris. It is sacred because it's the site of an annual ritual called the Turkey-Lurkey Bowl.

It's almost impossible to believe, but the first Turkey-Lurkey Bowl was played nearly fifteen years ago. My high school friends and I had recently graduated and scattered to colleges across the country. Parents and teachers had reassured us that we would soon make new, better friendships, that we would outgrow our adolescent ne'er-do-welling and discover more productive ways to spend our energies. All of this sounded terrifying to us. Defiant, we decided to hold a football game in Central Park on our first weekend back in town. We wouldn't tackle but would play "hard touch," which, despite its ring of sexual menace, simply meant that when you touched an opponent down, you could throw in a little shove for good measure. The idea was to make diving catches, pull off stutter-step jukes in the open field, and occasionally deliver punishing, ball-jarring body-blows. The idea was to prove that nothing had changed.

I should explain here that I didn't run with the jock crowd. Of the seven of us, six ranged from mildly uncoordinated to loafish and easily startled. A couple of us had been grudgingly granted spots on the junior varsity baseball team, but we quickly quit to work on the student newspaper. We'd never played with a professional-sized football before. Whenever I tried to pass, the ball wobbled in the air like a shot bird.

The problem was that the seventh member of our group, Nifty Johnson (I'll refer to players by their TLB nicknames), was our high school football team's starting quarterback. Granted, the football team didn't win a single game our senior year and, because the only wide receiver was very frightened of being tackled, the coach refused to call any pass plays. Still, Nifty could throw a spiral, he was twice as fast and strong as anyone else, and he actually knew receiver routes other than the bomb. He spoke with confidence about the Hook and Ladder, the Statue of Liberty, the Papa Smurf. (The rest of us are comfortable calling only two plays: the "Just Run Around a Lot" and the "Go Long, I Guess?") If Nifty was going to play, he'd have to be neutralized. Since we had an odd number of players, there was an easy solution: He would play quarterback for both teams. Running plays would be forbidden, because none of us could catch him.

For weeks we looked forward to the game, which we

decided we'd play on the day after Thanksgiving. We limited our family commitments to the holiday itself, and we called each other often to talk strategy. We hadn't yet picked the teams, but we were each certain that ours would win. We studied diagrams of bubble screens and end-arounds. I bought a pair of wristbands.

We chose the Dendur field because the parents of one of our friends, the Phantom, lived across the street; we figured we could use the apartment for a postgame locker room. But when the morning finally arrived, the Phantom, citing a mysterious back injury, canceled. We were stunned by this apparent betrayal, but we determined to go on anyway. The following year, 1999, the Phantom missed the game again, due to a sprained shoulder. The third year—TLBY2K—a groin. The Phantom's absence has now become a critical part of the ritual. He has not played in a single Turkey-Lurkey Bowl, despite the fact that he can see the field from his window. His excuse is different every year, but usually it has something to do with physical discomfort. He is in perfect health until someone mentions the football game, at which point he starts complaining of sharp pains.

The details of that first game—and for that matter the details of every subsequent game—blur. As ecstatic as it feels to cut sharply and break free of a defender, or to pluck an interception out of the air, the only specific plays I remember are those that have almost killed us. The most terrifying of these occurred during TLBY2K3. Mary Lou had somehow caught, over his shoulder, one of Nifty's gorgeous, high-arcing passes, without breaking stride. But his downfield momentum was so great that he went straight out of the east end zone, his stomach colliding with the short metal fence that blocks the field from the thirty-foot drop to the parking ramp. Fortunately Mary Lou's defender, close on his heels, alertly tackled him, pinning his body against the fence. Otherwise Mary Lou would have flipped over, head first, and that would have been the end of the Turkey-Lurkey Bowl.

One game stands out among the rest: the Mud Bowl (TL-BY2K). It had rained the night before so the field was even uglier than usual. There was no grass at all, only a slick, gelatinous fudge. It was like running on an oil slick. The slightest head fake from your opponent and you started skidding and slipping and sprawling face-first into the ground. Before long we were sopping brown, our faces inked like Amazonian warriors. The smell was atrocious, a mixture of body odor, liquidated feces (canine, we told ourselves), and wet turf. A dozen tourists in the Temple of Dendur exhibition gathered by the glass windows and watched us with expressions of admiration (the children) and disgust (the adults). On the way back to the subway we walked past a fire where a fireman took pity, spraying us down with a high-pressure firehose. It was pummeling and, being late November, very cold, but we were grateful.

The games are very close, with ties being common. Nifty's team doesn't win disproportionately, in large part because it's not enough to pass a ball—you also have to catch it. And the harder he pegs it, the less likely one of us will be able to hold on to it. The same six of us play every year, on the same teams. It is a Holy War—three Jews versus three Gentiles. It's also righties against lefties. (The Gentiles are all left-handed.) One year, early on, Nifty invited another friend, Androsalard, from our high school class. We all liked Androsalard. He's the most charming guy you'll ever meet. But we were so angry that the integrity of the ritual might be compromised that we forced Nifty, much to his shame, to disinvite him. None of us have seen Androsalard since.

We are as competitive as we are unskilled. Which is to say: monstrously. The Gentiles often meet beforehand to prepare strategy, while the Jews have a brief pregame pep talk in the west end zone, where they emphasize the importance of feigning confidence. Every year Squawkeye Squinge prepares a new taunting touchdown dance; in TLBY2K10 it was the Squawkeye Shuffle, which combines birdlike arm flapping with a slow, sensuous swivel of the hips. Chewy sometimes shows up wearing a T-shirt on which is printed a version of the No Smoking logo, only instead of a cigarette being crossed out, it's my name (not my nickname, my actual name). And there is usually a moment every game when Mary Lou, who in normal life is as considerate and gentle as any mother would want her son to be, releases a primal roar that turns heads on Fifth Avenue. It is a startlingly masculine, even violent sound, which seems to come from some deep chamber of his soul. The roar usually comes late in the game, after Mary has been shoved one too many times, and he has managed to make a reception despite being battered by several pairs of clumsy arms.

It seems strange that the Turkey-Lurkey Bowl, a ritual

devoted to our friendship, is the only day of the year when real animosity exists between us. The games don't start out aggressive, but after several series there has been enough shame and enough collisions with the glass wall of the Dendur gallery that we begin to feel genuine anger. Squabbling over the spot of the ball, pulling opponents' clothing as they run, and hurling the ball down the hill in frustration are common occurrences. It's the only time we curse—obscenely and without irony—at each other. But I've decided this is a necessary, even valuable part of the ritual. Not because it's cathartic, or because it allows lurking irritations to be aired in a healthy way, though that might be part of it. It's important because it is a crucial part of the transformation that we undergo as soon as we climb the hill to the Dendur plateau.

I wouldn't say that we become kids again, because, in a certain sense, let's face it, we're still kids; we belong to a generation for which childhood has yet to end. Despite being in our fourth decade, none of us is married or close to having our own children, only one of us has an office job, and many of us live communally, hand-to-mouth, in squalid dorms on the campus that is L-train Brooklyn. But the Bowl is still a form of regression, an expression of the emotions that tie us to each other.

Another year passes, but we end up in the same place. Our style of play hasn't improved, and the physical pain seems to be greater. After last year's game, TLBY2K10, I didn't leave my bed for two days. It wasn't the pain that kept me there, though it felt as if I'd survived a car crash—vertebrae spasms, a pair of sprained ankles, and, though my throwing shoulder throbbed, my other shoulder, inexplicably, was paralyzed. I was prepared for the pain, which has become as essential to the experience as the Phantom's no-shows. But I wasn't prepared for the exhaustion. My body, in shock, mistook the three-hour burst of exertion for a close brush with death, probably assuming that I'd barely survived being chased through the jungle by a tiger, or escaped an invading horde of barbarians. My survival instinct clicked in. During those two days I slept nearly thirty hours, and lay on my face, groaning, for at least another ten.

Other changes are under way. Nifty's hips have become arthritic and creaky. Chewy and Thumper, who defend each other, no longer pretend to run, and now rarely break into more than a light jog. And this year, at a particularly tense moment in the game, we were interrupted by jeers from down the hill. A group of boys, wearing backpacks and ballooning jeans, were razzing us.

"Oooh, throw me the ball," one of them called out.

"Can we play?" asked another, in a sarcastic, ingratiating tone.

For a second we were silent, surprised by this interruption. Then we started yelling back. The boys didn't seem especially intimidated, but they giggled and moved on. We laughed, but I think we were all shaken by the experience. We realized that those boys—those children—were the same age we were when we held the first Turkey-Lurkey Bowl.

No matter how our lives change, we'll keep playing. The Bowl is as much a part of Thanksgiving as tinfoil-wrapped leftovers. And when we have our own children, and they're old enough, we'll let them join us on the Dendur plateau. But they won't be allowed to play. No way. They can find their own damn field. This one is ours.

PAUL AUSTER
Fogg in the Park

I T HAD BEEN one thing to sit in my room and wait for the sky to fall on top of me, but it was quite another to be thrust out into the open. Within ten minutes of leaving the theater, I finally understood what I was up against. Night was approaching, and before too many more hours had passed, I would have to find a place to sleep. Remarkable as it seems to me now, I had not given any serious thought to this problem. I had assumed that it would somehow take care of itself, that trusting in blind dumb luck would be sufficient. Once I began to survey the prospects around me, however, I saw how dismal they really were. I was not going to stretch out on the sidewalk like some bum, I said to myself, lying there for the whole night wrapped in newspapers. I would be exposed to every madman in the city if I did that; it would be like inviting someone to slit my throat. And even if I wasn't attacked, I was sure to be arrested for vagrancy. On the other hand, what possibilities for shelter did I have? The thought of spending the night in a flophouse repulsed me. I couldn't see myself lying in a room with a hundred down-and-outs, having to breathe their smells, having to listen to the grunts of old men buggering each other. I wanted no part of such a place, not even if I could get in for free. There were the subways, of course, but I knew in advance that I would never be able to close my eyes down there—not with the lurching and the noise and the fluorescent lights, not when I thought some transit cop might be coming along at any moment to crash his nightstick against the soles of my feet. I wandered around in a funk for several hours, trying to come to a decision. If I eventually chose Central Park, it was only because I was too exhausted to think of anything else. At about eleven o'clock I found myself walking down Fifth Avenue, absently running my hand along the stone wall that divides the park from the street. I looked over the wall, saw the immense, uninhabited park, and realized that nothing better was going to present itself to me at that hour. At the very worst, the ground would be soft in there, and I welcomed the thought of lying down on the grass, of being able to make my bed in a place where no one could see me. I entered the park somewhere near the Metropolitan Museum, trekked out toward the interior for several minutes, and then crawled under a bush. I wasn't up to looking any more carefully than that. I had heard all the horror stories about Central Park, but at that moment my exhaustion was greater than my fear. If the bush didn't keep me hidden from view, I thought, there was always my knife to defend myself with. I bunched up my leather jacket into a pillow, then squirmed around for a while as I tried to get comfortable. As soon as I stopped moving, I heard a cricket chirp in an adjacent shrub. Moments later, a small breeze began to rustle the twigs and slender branches around my head. I didn't know what to think anymore. There was no moon in the sky that night, not a single star. Before I remembered to take the knife out of my pocket, I was fast asleep.

I woke up feeling as though I had slept in a boxcar. It was just past dawn, and my entire body ached, my muscles had turned into knots. I extricated myself gingerly from the bush, cursing and groaning as I moved, and then took stock of my surroundings. I had spent the night at the edge of a softball field, sprawled out in the shrubbery behind home plate. The field was situated in a shallow dip of land, and at that early hour a speckle of thin gray fog was hanging over the grass. Absolutely no one was in sight. A few sparrows swooped and chittered in the area around second base, a blue jay rasped in the trees overhead. This was New York, but it had nothing to do with the New York I had always known. It was devoid of associations, a place that could have been anywhere. As I turned this thought over in my mind, it suddenly occurred to me that I had made it through the first night. I would not say that I rejoiced in the accomplishment—my body hurt too much for that—but I knew that an important piece of business had been put behind me. I had made it through the first night, and if I had done it once, there was no reason to think I couldn't do it again.

I slept in the park every night after that. It became a sanctuary for me, a refuge of inwardness against the grinding demands of the streets. There were eight hundred and forty acres to roam in, and unlike the massive gridwork of buildings and towers that loomed outside the perimeter, the park offered me the possibility of solitude, of separating myself from the rest of the world. In the streets, everything is bodies and commotion, and like it or not, you cannot enter them without adhering to a rigid protocol of behavior. To walk among the crowd means never going faster than anyone else, never lagging behind your neighbor, never doing anything to disrupt the flow of human traffic. If you play by the rules of this game, people will tend to ignore you. There is a particular glaze that comes over the eyes of New Yorkers when they walk through the streets, a natural and perhaps necessary form of indifference to others. It doesn't matter how you look, for example. Outrageous costumes, bizarre hairdos, T-shirts with obscene slogans printed across them—no one pays attention to such things. On the other hand, the way you act inside your clothes is of the utmost importance. Odd gestures of any kind are automatically taken as a threat. Talking out loud to yourself, scratching your body, looking someone directly in the eye: these deviations can trigger off hostile and sometimes violent reactions from those around you. You must not stagger or swoon, you must not clutch the walls, you must not sing, for all forms of spontaneous or involuntary behavior are sure to elicit stares, caustic remarks, and even an occasional shove or kick in the shins. I was not so far gone that I received any treatment of that sort, but I saw it happen to others, and I knew that a day might eventually come when I wouldn't be able to control myself anymore. By contrast, life in Central Park allowed for a much broader range of variables. No one thought twice if you stretched out on the grass and went to sleep in the middle of the day. No one blinked if you sat under a tree and did nothing, if you played your clarinet, if you howled at the top of your lungs. Except for the office workers who lurked around the fringes of the park at lunch hour, the majority of people who came in there acted as if they were on holiday. The same things that would have alarmed them in the streets were dismissed as casual amusements. People smiled at each other and held hands, bent their bodies into unusual shapes, kissed. It was live and let live, and as long as you did not actively interfere with what others were doing, you were free to do what you liked.

There is no question that the park did me a world of good. It gave me privacy, but more than that, it allowed me to pretend that I was not as bad off as I really was. The grass and the trees were democratic, and as I loafed in the sunshine of a late afternoon, or climbed among the rocks in the early evening to look for a place to sleep, I felt that I was blending into the environment, that even to a practiced eye I could have passed for one of the picnickers or strollers around me. The streets did not allow for such delusions. Whenever I walked out among the crowds, I was quickly shamed into an awareness of myself. I felt like a speck, a vagabond, a pox of failure on the skin of mankind. Each day, I became a little dirtier than I had been the day before, a little more ragged and confused, a little more different from everyone else. In the park, I did not have to carry around this burden of self-consciousness. It gave me a threshold, a boundary, a way to distinguish between the inside and the outside. If the streets forced me to see myself as others saw me, the park gave me a chance to return to my inner life, to hold on to myself purely in terms of what was happening inside me. It is possible to survive without a roof over your head, I discovered, but you cannot live without establishing an equilibrium between the inner and outer. The park did that for me. It was not quite a home, perhaps, but for want of any other shelter, it came very close.

Unexpected things kept happening to me in there, things that seem almost impossible to me as I remember them now. Once, for example, a young woman with bright red hair walked up to me and put a five-dollar bill in my hand—just like that, without any explanation at all. Another time, a group of people invited me to join them on the grass for a picnic lunch. A few days after that, I spent the whole afternoon playing in a softball game. Considering my physical condition at the time, I turned in a creditable performance (two or three singles, a diving catch in left field), and whenever my team was at bat, the other players kept offering me things to eat and drink and smoke: sandwiches and pretzels, cans of beer, cigars, cigarettes. Those were happy moments for me, and they helped to carry me through some of the darker stretches when my luck seemed to have run out. Perhaps that was all I had set out to prove in the first place: that once you throw your life to the winds, you will discover things you had never known before, things that cannot be learned under any other circumstances. I was half-dead from hunger, but whenever something good happened to me, I did not attribute it to chance so much as to a special state of mind. If I was able to maintain the proper balance between desire and indifference, I felt that I could somehow will the universe to respond to me. How else was I to judge the extraordinary acts of generosity that I experienced in Central Park? I never asked anyone for anything, I never budged from my spot, and yet strangers were continually coming up to me and giving me help. There must have been some force emanating from me into the world, I thought, some indefinable something that made people want to do this. As time went on, I began to notice that good things happened to me only when I stopped wishing for them. If that was true, then the reverse was true as well: wishing too much for things would prevent them from happening. That was the logical consequence of my theory, for if I had proven to myself that I could attract the world, then it also followed that I could repel it. In other words, you got what you wanted only by not wanting it. It made no sense, but the incomprehensibility of the argument was what appealed to me. If my wants could be answered only by not thinking about them, then all thoughts about my situation were necessarily counterproductive. The moment I began to embrace this idea, I found myself staggering along an impossible tightrope of consciousness. For how do you not think about your hunger when you are always hungry? How do you silence your stomach when it is constantly calling out to you, begging to be filled? It is next to impossible to ignore such pleas. Time and again, I would succumb to them, and once I did, I automatically knew that I had destroyed my chances of being helped. The result was inescapable, as rigid and precise as a mathematical formula. As long as I worried about my problems, the world would turn its back on me. That left me no choice but to fend for myself, to scrounge, to make the best of it on my own. Time would pass. A day, two days, perhaps even three or four, and little by little I would purge all thoughts of rescue from my mind, would give myself up for lost. It was only then that any of the miraculous occurrences ever took place. They always struck like a bolt from the blue. I could not predict them, and once they happened, there was no way I could count on seeing another. Each miracle was therefore always the last miracle. And because it was the last, I was continually being thrown back to the beginning, continually having to start the battle all over again.

I spent a portion of every day looking for food in the park. This helped to keep expenses down, but it also allowed me to postpone the moment when I would have to venture into the streets. As time went on, the streets were what I came to dread most, and I was willing to do almost anything to avoid them. The weekends were particularly helpful in that regard. When the weather was good, enormous numbers of people came into the park, and I soon learned that most of them had something to eat while they were there: all manner of lunches and snacks, stuffing themselves to their hearts' content. This inevitably led to waste, gargantuan quantities of discarded but edible food. It took me a while to adjust, but once I accepted the idea of putting things into my mouth that had already touched the mouths of others, I found no end of nourishment around me. Pizza crusts, fragments of hot dogs, the butt ends of hero sandwiches, partially filled cans of soda—the meadows and rocks were strewn with them, the trash bins were fairly bursting with the abundance. To undercut my squeamishness, I began giving funny names to the garbage cans. I called them cylindrical restaurants, pot-luck dinners, municipal care packages—anything that could deflect me from saying what they really were. Once, as I was rummaging around in one of them, a policeman came up to me and asked what I was doing. I stammered for a few moments, completely caught off guard, and then blurted out that I was a student. I was working on an urban studies project, I said, and had spent the entire summer doing statistical and sociological research on the contents of city garbage cans. To back up my story, I reached into my pocket and pulled out my Columbia I.D. card, hoping that he wouldn't notice it had expired in June. The policeman studied the picture for a moment, looked at my face, studied the picture again for comparison, and then shrugged. Just be sure you don't put your head in too far, he said. You're liable to get stuck in one if you don't watch out.

I don't mean to suggest that I found this pleasant. There was no romance in stooping for crumbs, and whatever novelty it might have had in the beginning quickly wore off. I remembered a scene from a book I had once read, *Lazarillo de Tormes*, in which a starving hidalgo walks around with a toothpick in his mouth to give the impression that he had just eaten a large meal. I began affecting the toothpick disguise myself, always making a point to grab a fistful of them when I went into a diner for a cup of coffee. They gave me something to chew on in the blank periods between meals, but they also added a certain debonair quality to my appearance, I thought, an edge of self-sufficiency and calm. It wasn't much, but I needed all the props I could find. It was especially difficult to approach a garbage can when I felt that others were watching me, and I always made an effort to be as discreet as possible. If my hunger generally won out over my inhibitions, that was because my hunger was simply too great. On several occasions, I actually heard people laughing at me, and once or twice I saw small children pointing in my direction, telling their mothers to look at the silly man who was eating garbage. Those are things you never forget, no matter how much time has passed. I struggled to keep my anger under control, but I can recall at least one episode in which I snarled so fiercely at a little boy that he burst into tears. By and large, however, I managed to accept these humiliations as a natural part of the life I was living. In my strongest moods, I was able to interpret them as spiritual initiations, as obstacles that had been thrown across my path to test my faith in myself. If I learned how to overcome them, I would eventually reach a higher stage of consciousness. In my less exultant moods, I tended to look at myself from a political perspective, hoping to justify my condition by treating it as a challenge to the American way. I was an instrument of sabotage, I told myself, a loose part in the national machine, a misfit whose job was to gum up the works. No one could look at me without feeling shame or anger or pity. I was living proof that the system had failed, that the smug, overfed land of plenty was finally cracking apart.

Thoughts like these took up a large portion of my waking hours. I was always acutely conscious of what was happening to me, but no sooner would something happen than my mind would respond to it, blazing up with incendiary passion. My head burned with bookish theories, battling voices, elaborate inner colloquies. Later on, after I had been rescued, Zimmer and Kitty kept asking me how I had managed to do nothing for so many days. Hadn't I been bored? they wondered. Hadn't I found it tedious? Those were logical questions, but the fact was that I never became bored. I was subject to all kinds of moods and emotions in the park, but boredom wasn't one of them. When I wasn't busy with practical concerns (looking for a place to sleep at night, taking care of my stomach), I seemed to have a host of other activities to pursue. By midmorning, I was generally able to find a newspaper in one of the trash bins, and for the next hour or so I would assiduously comb its pages, trying to keep myself abreast of what was happening in the world. The war continued, of course, but there were other events to follow as well: Chappaquiddick, the Chicago Eight, the Black Panther trial, another moon landing, the Mets. I tracked the spectacular fall of the Cubs with special interest, marveling at how thoroughly the team had unraveled.

It was difficult for me not to see correspondences between their plunge from the top and my own situation, but I did not take any of it personally. When it came right down to it, I was rather gratified by the Mets' good fortune. Their history was even more abominable than the Cubs', and to witness their sudden, wholly improbable surge from the depths seemed to prove that anything in this world was possible. There was consolation in that thought. Causality was no longer the hidden demiurge that ruled the universe: down was up, the last was the first, the end was the beginning. Heraclitus had been resurrected from his dung heap, and what he had to show us was the simplest of truths: reality was a yo-yo, change was the only constant.

Once I had pondered the news of the day, I usually spent some time ambling through the park, exploring areas I had not visited before. I enjoyed the paradox of living in a man-made natural world. This was nature enhanced, so to speak, and it offered a variety of sites and terrains that nature seldom gives in such a condensed area. There were hillocks and fields, stony outcrops and jungles of foliage, smooth pastures and crowded networks of caves. I liked wandering back and forth among these different sectors, for it allowed me to imagine that I was traveling over great distances, even as I remained within the boundaries of my miniature world. There was the zoo, of course, down at the bottom of the park, and the pond where people rented small pleasure boats, and the reservoir, and the playgrounds for children. I spent a good deal of time just watching people: studying their gestures and gaits, thinking up life stories for them, trying to abandon myself totally to what I was seeing. Often, when my mind was particularly blank, I found myself lapsing into dull and obsessive games. Counting the number of people who passed a given spot, for example, or cataloguing faces according to which animals they resembled—pigs or horses, rodents or birds, snails, marsupials, cats. Occasionally, I jotted down some of these observations in my notebook, but for the most part I found little inclination to write, not wanting to remove myself from my surroundings in any serious way. I understood that I had already spent too much of my life living through words, and if this time was going to have any meaning for me, I would have to live in it as fully as possible, shunning everything but the here and now, the tangible, the vast sensorium pressing down on my skin.

SUSAN SHEEHAN
Sunday in the Park with Mother

W HEN I WAS young, I lived in an apartment on
East Seventy-ninth Street between First and Second
avenues with my mother and stepfather. When the three of
us, separately or together, set forth from the building, we
almost always turned left—westward—because there was
little of interest to the family between home and the East
River. The places that mattered were on Second Avenue
(Mertl's, the pork butcher, for outstanding cold cuts); Third
Avenue (Mrs. Herbst, purveyor of the finest strudel and Do-
bos torte in the Hungarian section of Yorkville); Lexington
Avenue (Womrath's bookstore, where my mother bought
me the latest volumes in the Cherry Ames, Beverly Gray, or
Nancy Drew series when a childhood illness like mumps
or chickenpox kept me home from school for two care-
free weeks); Park Avenue (my stepfather's medical office)
and what a pretty and double-wide thoroughfare it was,

especially at Christmas when lighted trees graced its me-
dian divide; Madison Avenue (Jane Engel, a boutique for
girls' clothes before *boutique* entered the American idiom);
and Fifth Avenue (the Metropolitan Museum of Art, where,
in the Egyptian wing, my mother wrapped bandages for
the Red Cross in the early 1940s). This was also, of course,
the block-by-block itinerary to Central Park, one of my
mother's favorite destinations, especially on Sundays,
when a sense of leisure prevailed over the city, in general,
and our lives, in particular.

My mother and I had been city people from the outset—
we were both born in Vienna—and we frequented parks
wherever we were. I have no memories of myself as an
eight-month-old in Austria, but in albums my mother kept
of my early years there are photographs of me in a chariot
of a pram in Vienna's Stadtpark, alongside my elegantly
dressed mother and a uniformed nanny, captioned in my
mother's unique handwriting, which my husband and our
daughters would struggle to decipher decades later. There are
photographs of me as a fourteen-month-old toddler in London's Kensington Gardens: same cast of characters, same
accoutrements. My father was obviously the photographer,
for there are far fewer pictures of him. He died in 1942, six
months after we set forth in a convoy from Edinburgh to
Montreal, and continued on by train to New York. I do not
remember him, and a year and a half later my mother married the man who had been her obstetrician in Vienna.

My earliest memories of Central Park are of the playgrounds close to Fifth Avenue to which I was taken when I

was a girl of five or six. It was there that I first experienced the up-and-down pleasures of seesaws; the hand-over-hand progress across monkey bars; clambering up jungle gyms; sitting on swings and learning to pump to fly ever higher up into the air and ever speedier back down. I recall my first few times ice-skating on the bumpy surfaces of one or another of Central Park's ponds and lakes, and that other wintertime pleasure: sledding down one of the two steep hills in the park between Seventy-second and Seventy-ninth streets on a sled painted red with silver trim, of unknown provenance, in a snowscape dominated by other children on blond birch Flexible Flyers.

My enduring memories of Central Park date from the mid-1940s, my grade-school years, when I was between seven and eleven. We went there infrequently during the week, when my mother was busy with bridge and canasta games and volunteer work, and I had school and a changing number of after-school activities: horseback riding and piano lessons and trips to the local public library, where I was allowed to borrow six books for a prescribed period of time, and always returned them and took out six others before that time was up. Saturdays were given over to more lessons (ballet) and to errands: It might be a visit to Mother's dressmaker, another to her milliner or her jeweler. Some lessons and errands were on the West Side of Manhattan, and on those days we simply transversed the park on foot or by bus. I can still remember my puzzlement at boarding the Seventy-ninth Street cross-town bus on East Seventy-ninth Street and exiting the park at Eighty-first Street and

Central Park West. It seemed a wayward itinerary for a bus. Other errands were downtown, and I took special pleasure in riding the green Fifth Avenue double-decker bus. We always climbed the stairs to the upper deck, perhaps because the buses that plied New York's other avenues were conventional one-story conveyances.

But Sunday—that was Central Park Day, and although we must have gone there dozens of times, those Sundays in the park with Mother had a joyful sameness. The weather surely varied, but in memory it is quite sunny and cool but not cold. We are dressed in jackets or coats. I am carrying a paper bag of three-day-old bread for feeding the birds. If we are walking, I scatter the breadcrumbs, in the manner of Hansel and Gretel, on the six-sided pavement stones that are to be found on the west side of Fifth. (In future years, when I see movies filmed in New York, the scene setters will not be just the Empire State Building, the Chrysler Building, and the Statue of Liberty, but those hexagonal pavers.) My pockets are filled with cubes of sugar for the horses I hope to encounter in the park or on the way there and back (and often did).

Horses still pulled ragpickers' carts on cobblestoned Second Avenue and on trolley-tracked Third Avenue under the el. Men and women rode rented steeds on the park's bridal paths, and occasionally I had serendipitous encounters with police horses or with Central Park West–based horses pulling carriages on one or another of the roads that wended through the park. I flattened my hand and proffered the contents of my pockets; their bits clinked as they munched, and I stroked their velvet muzzles.

My favorite place in Central Park, perhaps in the world when I was seven, was the Central Park Zoo. The first attraction, close to the Sixty-fourth Street entrance, was the sea lion pond. While I admired the glistening bodies of the sleek mammals gliding on the surface of the water and disappearing below it, then surfacing to leap gracefully above it, often while barking, clowning, and clapping their fins, it was the display case on one side of the metal gated fence surrounding the pond that made the deepest impression on me. Arrayed in the case were a collection of sharp objects; some appeared to be pointy rocks, but most resembled arrowheads. According to a label on the case, the objects had been thrown into the pond and had severely injured or killed sea lions. Showcasing these objects perplexed me. Did the zoo authorities think that offering up graphic illustrations of evil would protect these glorious creatures? I had a sad feeling the opposite was true. The murder of Central Park sea lions was my first conscious example of the evil that lurked in my sheltered world.

My mother thought that I should see all the other zoological sights once we were at Sixty-fourth and Fifth. The one that drew me on every zoo expedition was the monkey house. My mother did not care for aroma of monkey, so she accompanied me to the entrance door of the building and was always at the exit door waiting until I'd had my fill of the funny-faced varieties of lesser and greater apes swinging around their cages, eating bananas, chattering, and addressing each other noisily in the smelly heat.

The zoo was small, so we covered it from birds to bears

in an hour and then had lunch at the zoo cafeteria. My mother always ordered two cheeseburgers. We took them out to a terrace, and she ate the meat and cheese patty and half the bun: Mother always watched her figure. She drank a cup of black coffee, and, this being always Sunday, did the crossword puzzle in the *New York Times* Sunday magazine she had brought from home. After learning that *emu* was a large Australian bird and acquiring a sizable number of additional short two-vowel crossword-puzzle nouns while wolfing down everything on my plate, I fed my mother's remaining half bun to the birds that flocked onto and under the tables, seeking handouts. Central Park was the only place I knew of in the city with water fountains, and I saved some crumbs for the pigeons gathered in proximity to them. Sometimes my mother bought me sacks of peanuts and let me feed the park's importunate squirrels.

Now and again she took me to a section of the zoo where, for a few years, pony rides were offered; after these were discontinued, there were rides to be had in pony carts, but these seemed too tame. At other times we walked to the nearby merry-go-round. Even at six, I had disdained riding in the stationary wagons (those, I decided, were for little kids, usually accompanied by grown-ups riding with them; Mother never rode a merry-go-round) or on the stationary horses. I always insisted on climbing up on a large horse on the outermost ring of the carousel that rose up and down to the music. There my braveness ended: I never quite got up the courage to make serious attempts at grabbing the brass ring.

We usually made our way home from the zoo on foot (my mother believed, really believed, that exercise was a virtue), although sometimes she had brought my clamp-on roller-skates to the park and I used the key to affix them to my saddle shoes and skated home while she walked. I liked skating on the flat and slightly uphill stretches of sidewalk on Fifth, but dreaded the steep decline from the corner of Park Avenue toward Lexington on the east side of Seventy-ninth, where I stumbled on the rough squares and often fell hard; the scars on my knees have never gone away.

Those Central Park outings with Mother came to an end in 1948, after I graduated from PS 190, on East Eighty-second Street between First and Second avenues, and entered Hunter College Junior High School, at Sixty-eighth Street and Lexington. I had just turned eleven and was considered old enough to range more freely on my own during the week. On Saturdays in winter my classmates and I sometimes went to Broadway shows (then $1.20 to $1.80 for balcony seats) or, after it opened, went skating at Central Park's Wollman Rink. Hunter was hard, with five major subjects during high school except junior year, when we had six. Sundays were for homework.

Flash forward. Flash forward very far and very fast. I went to college in Massachusetts. I returned to New York City and became a writer. I moved away—to Indonesia (where I was married) and later to Vietnam (where I wrote my first book) and then to Washington, D.C.: My husband, Neil, had been transferred there by the *New York Times* to cover the Pentagon. Our two daughters, Maria and Catherine, were born, and before they went to school and during their school vacations we went to New York and stayed at my parents' apartment on East Seventy-ninth Street. Whenever I wasn't writing an article for "Talk of the Town" or researching a book, I relived parts of my childhood with them. Mertl's, Mrs. Herbst, Womrath's, Jane Engel, the cobblestones on Second Avenue, the trolleys on Third, and the Third Avenue el, as well as Fifth Avenue's double-deckers were long gone, but Central Park offered an array of new delights, among them the Children's Zoo, replete with alpacas, llamas, and sheep, and the Delacorte Musical Clock. Two bronze monkeys atop the Roman numeraled clock, metal mallets in paws, banged the time on a bell on the hour and half hour, followed by a band of six whimsical animals (including a bear with a tambourine and an elephant playing a concertina), which glided and rotated around a track to the accompaniment of nursery rhyme tunes and songs from Broadway musicals.

Time keeps ticking away, on plain and fanciful clocks. It is Saturday, the twelfth of June, 2010. At half after five o'clock the daughter of cherished friends is married at Central Presbyterian Church at Park Avenue and Sixty-fourth Street. After the wedding ceremony, Neil and I walk with the other guests to the reception at the Central Park Zoo. We pass the sea lion pond—remodeled since my childhood and with discreetly posted reminders that coins can kill the animals, but with no egregious coin exhibit. The late afternoon is warm and so, iced drinks in hand, we enter the chilled domain of the puffins and penguins, and watch the elegantly tailored, intrinsically comical black-and-white seabirds waddling about until it is time for dinner at flower-bedecked tables set up close by. We raise our glasses to the young couple, and on the way back to the hotel Neil and I speak of the fun we will have in 2011 taking our three-year-old grandson on his first excursion to the ever-changing, ever-magical place that is Central Park.

THOMAS BELLER
Negative Space

1

MAYBE IT WAS because it took place on the gorgeous promenade that during the day feels so stately and European, with its huge trees interspersed with a parade of statues, heavy-duty thinking men, all of them exuding Rodin-like on-the-john contemplative authority, the whole thing funneling into the Naumburg Bandshell and beyond it the Bethesda Fountain and the Lake, or maybe it was because we were young kids, angry at some insult we could not really name, the prolonged insult of being fourteen and not getting anything and wanting so much, but the guy who antagonized us that night, a dark silent summer night, would need to be reprimanded, punished, his act accounted for, this was clear. So we circled back in a long arc to the start of the promenade, the two of us poised like drag racers while the offending party, the enemy, walked alone, his back to us, unsuspecting, a solitary figure in our sights.

We came to this agreement, Adrian and I, without saying much. Adrian was a stoic. He was in constant touch with the ever-flickering scoreboard of fate and karma from which he got important information through telepathy. I tended to shut up around him, the better to let the silence creep in and provide a kind of black velvet pulpit from which he would speak his few, profound words, or I would speak my more copious, less profound ones. Somehow it was agreed that because the guy was walking right down the middle of the promenade we would both charge on either side, coming from behind. We did not actually intend to attack him. We were not even going to touch him. Like two fighter planes roaring in formation, we would merely buzz him on either side and disappear into the enveloping darkness of the park.

We started, each mounted on our respective bikes, slowly, picking up speed, and soon were flying. The target was in our sights. When he heard us he turned around.

Who was he? What was he doing by himself in the park at night? What were we doing in the park? Most important, what had he done to piss us off? I have no idea. I just know we were antagonized, out late, summertime exploring, and had found ourselves where we spent so much time, the park, down in that sweet spot where the Great Lawn was, and the Bandshell, and the Bethesda Fountain, and the Lake, the spooky brambles nearby.

He turned and saw us, coming at him on either side. He ran at Adrian, who tried to steer clear, but couldn't. Adrian crashed into a bench. He was already braking like crazy, so it wasn't a violent crash, just kind of ignoble. I could tell from his body language that the first thing he wanted to do was check to see if his front wheel was damaged, but the guy was in his face. I came over. I remember all this, lit by those street lamps spaced at such dignified intervals, but it sits by itself with no context.

"What the fuck?" said Adrian.

"What do you mean 'what the fuck'?" said the guy. "What the fuck were you doing coming up on me like that? What the fuck!" But now I am veering into fiction.

What happened was Adrian and the guy got into a strange tangled argument about the ethics of the whole thing; Adrian, in the classic logic of a fourteen-year-old, arguing that he was not going to do anything, he was just biking fast, was there a law against biking fast? Et cetera. The guy pointing out, agitated, that two guys coming up on him fast on bikes whom he just had words with . . . but it again fades to black, a factless void, the scene illuminated only by one streetlight of memory that extends only as far as this scene.

It ended without blows. Surely we went home after. Was it one of the nights our mothers called each other anxiously, asking if the other one knew where we were? The memory vanishes. The year was 1979, I would guess. Or maybe 1980, the summer we were bike messengers. Old New York. Statistically much more dangerous than the New one. And also, somehow, more private. Maybe what we were arguing about, that dude and us, was the right to have the whole place to ourselves.

2

If you grow up in New York City, or maybe just Manhattan, as I did, you become a connoisseur of negative space. For hard-core city-philes—I mean the people who allow for the texture and topography of the city to enter their soul—these spaces are refuges, tiny oases, sought after, multipurpose. They are meditative temples. They are moments of rest.

There is so much action in New York one is sometimes perversely excited by those places where you are not part of it. Where nothing is happening. These places, in turn, become little air pockets of possibility. They are unidentified, off the grid, the staging areas for trysts, seductions, encounters. They are the places where crimes are committed, of one kind or another. The most conspicuous, hiding-in-plain-sight negative space in New York is Central Park.

3

There were four of us, the West Side freaks. Worth and I lived on Riverside Drive. John and Adrian lived on Central Park West. We attended a private school in the Riverdale section of the Bronx. Most of the kids in our school were ferried to school from Manhattan on private bus lines that picked everyone up at various points and then rumbled through Harlem, across the 133rd Street bridge, up the Major Deegan, past the Stella D'oro cookie factory with its useful clock on top and its fleeting whiff of sweetness, and at last into the verdant cloistered world of Riverdale. There were something like seven or eight buses that ran up the various East Side avenues. The West Side had two. One for Central Park West and one for West End.

We were West Side kids. I now look at my whole generation from that school, the rich, the sort of rich, and not so rich kids of private school Manhattan circa the 1970s and early '80s, as a group that had OD'd on affluence, safety, and prosperity. Also, despite a serious crime wave and depletion of city services, we were undoubtedly the last generation of kids who were allowed to roam around the city with relative autonomy, without the specter of Amber alerts and 24-7 coverage of every abducted or missing young person in America stoking parental paranoia, fantasy, and guilt. Being on a long leash in the city at the age of ten or eleven was unremarkable.

We were bingers and a bit manic, and we were surrounded by the iconography of ruin. The city itself had just survived a near-death experience. You didn't have to actually see and comprehend the famous *Daily News* headline FORD TO CITY: DROP DEAD! to sense it in the air. When you're a kid, pending anarchy is something you root for. It means school is out. All bets are off. That the city was in a state of extreme dishevelment complicated and added to this manic behavior. I'd like to say it made my peers and I, on some level, feel guilty about our good fortune, but that was not the case. Rather it made everyone into a barbarian, sacking an already crumbling world for fun. We were destroyers.

We had been blessed with excess. Being children, we had no sense of what preceded it. Our visceral response was to take all the excess and break it, deface it, when possible, burn it to the ground.

There was a lot of severing. Within our West Side gang three of us were children of divorce. Of those three, two were living with stepfathers with whom relations were frosty. One lived with his mother and brother, but the father's temperamental presence lingered like the smell of his cigarettes; the shiny purple wallpaper of that apartment's enormous rooms seemed, to me, to be the color of secrets.

The one kid who was not a child of divorce was me. My father died when I was ten, a year or two before we all started to hang out. The group's tightness lasted into the first year or so of high school. All of us lived on a park.

Riverside Park was a splendid place for adventure, an excellent playground resource, a good place to go by yourself to throw a tennis ball against a wall, and the setting for the formative basketball court of my life, on Seventy-seventh Street, which still thrives.

But Riverside Park did not pull you in. It had none of the glamour, the gravitational pull, of Central Park. When you were in an apartment that overlooked Riverside Park, your eye went to the river, the astonishing fact of it, its breadth and flatness. Then you examined the fairly hideous

New Jersey coast, also astonishing in its own way, and then your gaze went back to the river. You didn't spend much time gazing down into Riverside Park.

Adrian and John, the two Central Park West kids, were usually the hosts among our group. Some of this was due to the simple fact that their apartments were bigger. But some of it, also, was due to the proximity of Central Park.

If you were in an apartment that overlooked Central Park, as Adrian's did, you stared at the park. You stared at the thing itself and also the weird neatness of its parameters. The way it set itself off so completely from the city into which it had been dropped. Later on I came to understand the grand accomplishment of the park's design, the hugely artificial nature of its terrain. But as a kid staring into it from above, I couldn't help but feel that the park itself was the original terra firma of the city which had somehow been given exterior walls, like a fort, around which the city grew. What was inside the walls was a kind of original sin of nature. To have a view of it was to have access to a strange kingdom. You became entranced by the intricate patterns of its winding paths. By the weather systems that seemed to exist over the park alone.

When I first saw, through an airplane window, the Lost Kingdom of Angkor Wat, in northern Cambodia, its territory sharply set off in a symmetrical rectangle of stone from the mass of surrounding jungle, my first thought was of the view of Central Park from above, the way it too was a world delineated sharply from its surroundings. Like Angkor, it was a kingdom of its own.

Adrian's place was on Eighty-ninth Street, so there was also opportunity for close examination of the Reservoir: Its strange, faintly kidney shape. The shushing patterns of light. The ripples pulling across the surface in one direction and then another, revealing the invisible, unheard wind. The little scampering bodies jogging around its perimeter. Central Park was mystical. Across its expanse rose the Upper East Side, a formidable foe. We gazed at the park, we entered into it. We felt its pull. It was a kind of no-man's-land, a place of possibility. It was a negative space.

4

We were into skateboards. It amazes me to think of this— my membership in early skateboard culture. When it came roaring back, whenever that was, the early 1990s, and became, like surfing, a permanent annex to the world of cool, I was impatient for it to come and go. I didn't dislike it. I just thought, *we did that already.* I could never have guessed at how enduring it would be. I didn't realize that twelve-year-olds through eternity would be thrilled by the feel of rolling.

That had been me at the time, with my West Side gang. I discussed trucks and boards. I partook in the great wheel debates about Road Runner versus Kryptonic. The latter were soft and looked like candy, but I preferred the former, fours on the back and twos on the front. I had opinions about trucks. I want to say my board was Fibreflex, but I think that was the name of my sled.

Mostly, I used my skateboard to get places. Skateboarding down a street, you occupied a kind of negative space between the world of pedestrians and cars. Later, I came to think of it as a gateway drug to my next phase of negative space transportation, the bicycle.

As a group, we would spend weekend afternoons skateboarding the hill next to John's apartment. The spot provided several unique amenities. One was a long, curving hill which began around Sixty-eighth Street, near the Great Lawn, and swung down past Seventy-second Street, leaving you at the bottom of another hill at the top of which was the Bethesda Fountain and the Bandshell, the physical and spiritual center of all youthful parkie dereliction.

The spot's biggest draw, however, was the horse-drawn carriages. We would start at the top and slalom down amid the crowds of people and the piles of horseshit. The carriage's route was counterclockwise through the park, which is to say, back up the hill we had just come down.

At the bottom we would loiter until a carriage went by. There were massive bongo drum circles nearby, a blizzard of bongo beats and cowbells, guys standing with a jug of Bacardi at the end of an outstretched arm, bandana around their neck or head, whooping. It was like skateboarding down into a mad party. We'd let it pour over us until a carriage passed. On nice weekend days the wait was never more than a few minutes. Then we would skate up behind it, crouch down, and grab hold of the rear axle, or whatever was down there to grab. Staying crouched low was important. You had to be able to see the piles of horseshit, both old and new, that dotted the road, and avoid them. Also, the driver often knew we were there, and would flip his whip back over the carriage. By some fateful miracle these whips always snapped just above our heads. But they snapped with malice. They weren't warnings.

I always wondered how the driver explained this gesture to his passengers. I could never hear his voice. Only now and then, if the carriage was empty, would the driver yell at us. I don't recall any driver ever actually stopping. It didn't occur to us to feel sorry for the horse.

Because of the wrath of the driver, and his whip, a carriage with one person was ideal, two people was okay, and three people was pushing it. Either way, we lived in giddy fear of the whip as we rode back up the hill.

In winter, our forays were less frequent but more dramatic. Snow days were surreal dreams, the snow day itself being pure negative space. The cancellation of school. The plunge into the whiteness with sleds. The eventual retreat to Adrian or John's place for hot chocolate.

The Blizzard of '77 (cue the Nada Surf song of the same name, written twenty-five years later and very evocative) was an epic of staggering through a white landscape, the place mostly empty. None of us ever said it, but I think the fantasy was that we were the last people alive on Earth. Why was Central Park mostly empty in the middle of a blizzard? Because it was a blizzard. But was it really empty? Did we go hours without seeing anyone except an occasional cross-country skier? All those arrival tracks zigzagging this way and that would suggest otherwise. But such is the glory of Central Park and its many nooks and crannies that at any given moment it holds thousands of people who feel like they are alone.

5

The difference between the Upper East Side and the Upper West Side used to be substantial. Now it is a question of subtle gradations. This lack of delineation is one of the weirdest changes to the psychic landscape of New York in the last twenty-five or so years. Today a visitor might wander through the park from one side to another and feel it was a kind of oasis in the midst of a continuous fabric, but in recent decades it also served as a kind of moat, a Maginot Line that separated two worlds and worldviews

And if the park was a kind of DMZ in which one could wander, there was also means to cross the border efficiently from one side to the next. No one asked for your passport. It was an interval of stopped time: the Central Park Transverse.

6

There are some things that I will only write in third person:

He ignores the bodies around him. It is the rush-hour crush, the after-school press. He is a teenager standing amid the bodies. One hand holds the bar above his head. The other is open, hanging there, oblivious. Halfway through Central Park and the bus is careening. It has a momentum of its own, as though the bus is a pinball, hitting the curves at speed. The passengers are inside, packed, spinning.

Gravity delivers an ass cheek into his palm. His body understands this before his mind can process the fact. A woman's ass has fallen into his open, blameless hand. Its shape matches the curve of his palm. The fabric of the dress is light, a tiny filament separating his hand from the thing itself. Then the bus swerves, and gravity takes away what it had given him.

He is twelve. He is there. She is there. A lot of other people are on the bus, too, but the world has narrowed to his hand, her body. They stand back-to-back. The bus rolls as it takes a curve through the tunnel, and the ass cheek is disengaged.

Those mysterious tunnels. Some have ceilings lined with elegant brick. Others look as if a giant had bitten a mouthful of rock, chewed, and built a tunnel out of the boulders he spat out.

Exterior. Day. Bus shoots into a tunnel.

Interior. Bus. The many faces in light, suddenly thrown into darkness. It lasts a blink. It mimics, for a second, the effect of the flickering lights of a subway car.

Exterior. Day. Bus shoots out of dark tunnel, speeding, impatient cars packed in a tight line behind it.

It takes another curve, and the ass cheek is back.

This is before the Grumman buses arrived, those sleek behemoths with the snub noses that kneel and curtsey, emit deep, life-weary sighs at every stop. This is a bus from *Dog Day Afternoon, Serpico, The Taking of Pelham 123*. A *French Connection* bus. A *Three Days of the Condor* bus.

The passengers tilt like a field of wheat blown by a gust of wind. The coming and going of the anonymous passenger's ass is as blameless a gesture as the soft slap of wake on pier after a boat has long since passed. He stares straight ahead. What is she staring at? Through the window he sees only the blocky stones of the transverse; up above them is the verdant green of the park. They are in a subterranean world. The negative space of the transverse.

A tiny sidewalk lines the road. Any time he sees someone walking on it, he feels pity for them, as though they are souls who have taken a wrong turn. A mistake, he thinks, anyone on that sidewalk has made a terrible mistake.

He stands there frantically trying to imagine what the woman behind him is thinking. He slowly turns his head and glimpses a young lady with curly hair down around her shoulders peering into a magazine. All he can see is a slender neck tilted down in concentration, unperturbed. Had she not even noticed his touch? Or is she standing there in a state of burning indignation, prevented from turning and accusing him only by the fact that the bus is now careening a little recklessly through the transverse's curves? Is she contemplating the difficulty and embarrassment of making a scene?

Then there is the delectable possibility that she felt the initial pat, the subsequent flip of the fingers, lifting the cheek up to shudder down, and then the final, gravity-aided pat, almost a light slap, in ways that defied the like/dislike axis spectrum and existed on another spectrum entirely—one of arousal, guilt, anger, fear. Which is to say, maybe she felt exactly as he did! Wasn't this the necessary atmosphere for the actual combustion of sex? He didn't know.

He goes into the fat boy swoon. This is an exaggerated version of a common fantasy of young boys, in which their friend's hot older sister, a freshman or sophomore in high school, anoints them worthy and delivers a kind of communion of sex: kneel and receive the gift. In this fantasy the woman descends like an angel. Sex is not conquest but an act of beneficence bequeathed by gods, a kind of philanthropy.

On the other hand, he thinks, maybe she is pissed as hell and he should bolt as soon as the doors open, before she has a chance to call the police.

In the negative space of the transverse, passing through and beneath the negative space of the park, he stands there in a state of terrified arousal.

The bus arrives at Broadway with a cranky, gasping grunt. He emerges onto the street, the enormous, almost punitive green Converse All Star book bag on his back. Broadway smells of Williams roast chicken. He never saw her face.

7

It was at night that my pleasure in Central Park was most acute. I liked to bike through it. For twelve years, starting at eighteen, I would bike from the Upper West Side to my social life in the East Village. In both directions, down and back, I went through the park. My route back home was Sixth Avenue. This was partly because it was the only north-bound avenue with a bike lane at the time. Partly because I love the spooky landscape of skyscrapers at night. And partly because it meant that the ride would culminate in entering the park at Fifty-ninth Street, rolling grandly through the park's lower reaches, past the lagoon whose ducks had been the source of Holden Caulfield's concern, and up into the gorgeous promenade, lined with lamps, which feels like a gorgeous haunted runway that leads you past the Bandshell and straight into the terrace above the Bethesda Fountain and the Lake behind it; I would exit at Seventy-second Street and relative proximity to home.

But I had my first encounters with the park at night before all that, when I was a kid, usually with Adrian or some combination of the West Side gang. There is one stretch of time that now emerges from the mist: For a week I was left alone at age fifteen. Alone in the apartment, but not to be trusted with a lump sum of money.

An arrangement was made. I commuted every other evening to my grandfather's place on the East Side. I did this at night. I never actually saw him or my grandmother. The envelope was left with the night doorman. He was old, with watery blue eyes, and I suppose he had seen me grow up. He wore white gloves and had a rim of white hair around his shiny bald head. I still remember the way he peeled off those gloves a couple of years later to shake my hand the night my grandfather died. For that week on my own, he was one of the most friendly faces I saw. He greeted me so warmly. After he handed me the envelope he saw me off with a big wave.

I would take the envelope to the steps of the brightly lit Metropolitan Museum to examine its contents. Then I would head home. On the way east, in eagerness, I took the transverse. But going home, I went through the park itself, tempting fate with my envelope.

There was one spot on the north end of the Great Lawn where I would pause to look at the skyline. Regarding the city from that vantage point, I felt small, like a stowaway, and kind of huge and powerful, too. The spangled lights, the huge towers, the movements of planes in the sky—it all created a vivid perimeter of brightness to the darkness of the park.

It was like staring at a partly cloudy sky at night, when after a while the patches of clouds and sky become confused, and you don't know which area is the hole in the clouds, and which area is the cloud itself. Which parts are far away but relatively near, and which parts are as far away as far can be—the bottomless black universe? This is a variation on the dream/reality problem. You know when you are awake and yet, especially when you are young, there is something about dreams, their vividness, that creates a doubt. Which is the real and which is the imagined? Where is the division between positive and negative space?

I felt this way about Central Park at night. When I was outside its borders it was a strange, mysterious territory. But once inside I nestled within it, felt cosseted, protected.

Everything beyond its boundaries was what seemed dangerous. I was inside a reality that protected me from reality. I loved the view from that spot at night. From inside the darkness I filled up on the power of negative space.

ALEC WILKINSON
The Hidden Life

F OR A LONG time I have been interested in the hidden life. Scenes that play across the imagination before sleep, the fleeting impressions one takes in from the corner of one's eye that are there and not there, reveries—anything that resides on the border of consciousness. I like it in all its guises and representations, and almost anywhere it shows up, but I am especially drawn to objects and places that are underground. The bottom of the ocean or a pond, or vaults of some kind. Underground rivers. Sometimes I see a documentary about the pyramids, and it takes days to shed the wish that I was among the people who first walked down those corridors with nothing but mysteries ahead of me.

For a while I had a hobby of visiting underground places in New York City such as train and subway tunnels; tunnels that I had heard were dug by bootleggers between their basements and the rivers; tunnels in Chinatown built during the Tong Wars for fighters to disappear into; a section of the aqueduct in the Bronx which someone told me went all the way to Manhattan (I managed one winter to squeeze into a part of it, but it ended after a few feet in a wall). I took a long subway and bus ride to the end of Brooklyn, where it plays out into marshland and sand dunes, and walked up a hill past gates that no longer worked to visit the desolate shoebox-shaped concrete spaces where surface-to-air missiles were kept during the 1950s and '60s. It was so far away from the rest of the city and so still and quiet that I might as well have been in the desert listening to the wind whistle.

By arrangement, I rode a slow, cage elevator down into the water tunnel being dug a mile below Queens. Because of the shape of the drill, the tunnel was a circle big enough for a bus to drive through, with tracks on the floor for a little train that took workers called sandhogs to the drill site. Another time I walked through an underground section of the New York Public Library on Forty-second Street that carried steam pipes and was sufficiently remote from the rest of the library that employees who lived in boarding-houses and did their laundry in sinks in the library basement hung it in the tunnel to dry.

One night I persuaded a friend who had bolt cutters to cut the lock on a chain that held a gated door closed over a tunnel in Central Park on the Eighty-sixth Street Transverse. I left the chain in place, so that it appeared to be intact, and the next night I came back and went through the doors. There was a long stone vaulted tunnel with a dirt floor leading to the basement of the pump house at the southern end of the Reservoir, which I explored for as long as I thought was safe, then I hotfooted it back to the street and walked as casually as I could to Fifth Avenue and hailed a taxi.

The largest underground space I visited was a chamber several stories beneath Central Park that had a high vaulted ceiling which made the place seem like a small cathedral. Within the room a number of water pipes intersected—it was a sort of switching station for the city's water supply— and the lights were always on. Water ran through seams in the walls from underground streams. To reach the room I had walked through the park to a brushed metal door in a stone wall with someone who worked for the city water authority. We took an elevator like one in an office build- ing, although there was also a set of stairs that wound in a deep spiral to a room outside the chamber. I like to cross the lawn above it, behind the Metropolitan Museum, and think that something like a hundred feet beneath me is a room with all the lights on.

The creatures that exemplify the hidden life for me are turtles, of which there are plenty in Central Park, especially in Turtle Pond, at the foot of the Great Lawn. I spent a lot of my childhood looking for turtles. They seemed to me to be deeply enigmatic, as if they knew some ancient and fun- damental secret, something from the dreamtime like aborigi- nes might know. I was very pleased when I learned of the Native American legend that assumes the world to be sup- ported on the back of a turtle, called the world turtle. It made sense to me. What other creature would have the wisdom or patience or majesty? I like the story, too, of the old woman who is supposed to have told William James that the earth was supported by a turtle. James asked her what the turtle was resting on, and she said another turtle. When he asked her what *that* turtle rested on, she said, I'm sorry, Mr. James, there's no use asking. It's turtles all the way down.

The turtles in the Turtle Pond are mainly, and perhaps entirely, thrown-out turtles. Generations of owners have abandoned them, when they felt they could no longer keep them, I guess, so you have breeds that you are not likely to find anywhere else in New York State, or even the Northeast. The most numerous breed is the red-eared slider, the green turtles with red stripes on their ears which pet stores sold as hatchlings, until it became illegal to, although sometimes you still see them in the fish stores in Chinatown. Their range is mainly southern—they live in the boat canal in Washington, D.C.—but not too much north of there. Like the parakeets that have escaped from shipments through Kennedy Airport and established colonies in Queens, they have thrived, despite the cold. I wonder if only the hardier ones have. I once let a pair of red-eared sliders go in a small pond on Cape Cod and kept a lookout for them but never saw them again. The climate doesn't favor them. A lot of unusual breeds show up in Turtle Pond, too. They remind me of the exotic fish that follow currents of warm water up the East Coast in the summer and end up wintering by the warm water outflow of the nuclear power plant up the

Hudson River. There is a false map turtle, which is a beautiful turtle, with a yellow streak on the side of its black head and an eye like a dark stone. I can't help wondering who brought it to New York and with what expectations and what it did to get the boot. It is not a turtle commonly sold as a pet, so someone went to some effort to acquire it, its range according to my copy of the *Encyclopedia of Turtles*, by Peter Pritchard, "extends from southern Minnesota and Wisconsin south to the Sabine River, which separates Louisiana from Texas." An exile dreaming of deep water and the wilderness is how I imagine it.

The turtles in the park to which I have the deepest attachment are the snapping turtles, of which I have seen at least two. The larger one is nearly the size of a café tabletop and moves like a battleship among the flotillas of smaller turtles that gather for handouts by the deck behind the Delacorte Theater. Snappers aren't rare, but they don't show up often in the wild. They're the Greta Garbo of turtles. They keep to the bottom and emerge only to breathe, unlike other turtles which bask. The big Central Park snapper is more sociable than any snapper in the wild would ever be. He (or she) is reserved to the point of politeness. Snapping turtles, like many other large creatures, are unaggressive; they attack only on land, where they venture to lay eggs and feel vulnerable. They live in dim light, like figures from the unconscious. I find comfort in knowing they are there in the park, because they represent my impression of the wild, as bears in a woods do. A pond with a snapping turtle is a complete pond, the way a woods with a bear or a big bird is complete.

A pond's appeal derives partly from the rising of things to its surface. We watch a pond waiting for something to happen. It is like waiting for thoughts to arrive. We don't watch the ocean that way or running water like a river. In those cases, it is the movement we follow, the waves or the current or the pools and knuckly ridges of water around a rock or downed tree. Somewhere I read that fire accelerates one's sense of time, and I think that a still surface of water does too, because of its imminence. Fire makes one aware of destruction and death, and the temporary quality of life. It speeds up existence and draws things to a quicker end. It makes passing time dramatic. It fascinates us, as does a still pond, although differently. Nothing startling seems ever to come to the surface of the ponds in Central Park, except perhaps the alligators that people dump in them every few years. The ponds are probably too filthy to be habitable by many species of fish and too small and crowded and shallow for any big predatory fish. And of course, they're landlocked. But the snapper comes to the surface in Central Park, and I feel fortunate when I see it.

When my son was five and six and seven and even older, he and I liked to go to Turtle Pond so he could sneak up on turtles that were sunning themselves on rocks or chum the water with bread crumbs and grab them. He would examine them for a little while, then he would put them back. This irritated other people, mostly, for some reason, women.

They would say, "That's a wild animal, you know, and he shouldn't disturb it." I would ignore them or say, "He's just being a kid in the city. Kids in the country catch turtles all the time." If one of them persisted, if she followed us, I would say, "Lady, you have any idea where these turtles come from? Did you think they had managed to cross a bridge and walk into Manhattan and avoid being run over and find this pond? They're thrown-out pets. That's why you can catch them so easily. They're *tame*." I'm making it sound like more fun than it actually was.

My son gave up catching turtles when he stuck his hand in the water and one bit him, breaking the skin, which at least proved to my satisfaction that although the water in the pond looks like it might carry typhoid, it doesn't.

Once I found a turtle in the middle of the East park drive, miraculously avoiding taxis. It was in the spring, and the turtle was looking for somewhere to lay its eggs, which is not easy given the amount of pavement and rock in the park. I picked it up—it was about the size of a hubcap—and walked it back to the water, with people looking at me as if I were trying deliberately to be provocative, like those guys who show up on spring and summer days with parrots on their shoulders or pythons around their necks. Another time my son and I were standing behind the Delacorte Theater, and he looked down, and at his feet was a hatchling painted turtle about the size of a quarter. I have no idea how it got there. It couldn't have walked that far. A bird might have picked it up and tried to eat it and dropped it.

My son took it back to the water. By now, if it survived, it would be about the size of a pancake.

The other hidden objects in Central Park that appeal to my imagination are the four boxes by Joseph Cornell that he buried in the vicinity of the Carousel in 1967. I know about them from Howard Hussey, an artist who was with him when he did it.

Cornell was deeply attached to his brother, Robert, who suffered in childhood from an affliction that was probably cerebral palsy. Robert lived his grown-up life in a wheelchair, and Cornell took care of him much of the time, until Robert died in 1965. Cornell believed in signs and omens and immaterial presences, and Hussey often had the feeling, sitting with Cornell in his house, that the reason Cornell's gaze sometimes left Hussey's face and focused on a place beyond one of his ears was that he saw Robert.

Cornell regarded Central Park as a mystical place, Hussey told me. He liked the Children's Zoo, and he liked to go to the main zoo with some tea in the afternoon and watch the seals being fed. One day he told Hussey that he wanted his help to bury four boxes in the park as a memorial to Robert. The boxes he chose were ones that Hussey had seen on a shelf in Cornell's studio and had wondered why they were never moved, while others were moved all the time.

Late one fall, around one in the morning, they took a taxi from Cornell's house on Utopia Parkway in Queens, not far from Kennedy Airport. Cornell had wrapped the boxes in heavy plastic, and in each one he had put a note to Robert. He brought a flat-edged shovel and a straight knife. He was worried that a policeman or a park worker might see them, but "it was a moonless night," Hussey said, "and we weren't revealed."

When they reached the place Cornell had selected, he got down on his knees and cut a long rectangle in the grass and lifted it like it was a quilt. With the shovel, he dug down about three feet, then placed the four boxes in the hole and covered them with dirt. "When we put the grass back, you couldn't tell that anything had been disturbed," Hussey said. They walked back to Fifth Avenue, and Cornell took a taxi home.

Hussey no longer lives in New York. When he comes to the city, he visits the place where the boxes are buried to make sure no one has disturbed them.

SUSAN CHEEVER
My Little Bit of Country

My EARLIEST MEMORIES are of summer mornings in Central Park with my father after he came home from fighting World War II in the Pacific with the gift of a bamboo hat for my mother and a lot of memories he never talked about. He would wear his khaki uniform with its boat-shaped hat and sergeant's stripes as we boarded the orange Fifty-ninth Street trolley car to the Central Park Zoo. At the zoo we were always greeted by our good friend Joe, who happened to be a chimpanzee. Joe had the run of the place, roller-skating on the asphalt paths past the lions and the seal pool in his Giants baseball jersey and sometimes even cavalierly smoking a stinky cigar.

My favorite animal at the zoo in those days before animal rights and civil rights and helicopter parents was the ancient yak who stood immovable in his outdoor cage just south of the great iron gates that are the entrance to the zoo. Something about him suggested a great acceptance of the world in which he found himself so far from his snowy native mountains and bubbling brooks. I too often felt, even then at the age of three or four, that I had come from another exotic foreign place to live with my disappointingly ordinary family in New York City at 400 East Fifty-ninth Street. The yak's endless forbearance inspired me. At night I dreamed that the yak stood impassively on the other side of the white bars of my crib.

The city in those years just after the war was a romantic place, a place of dreams and the beginnings of prosperity for people like my young parents. My father was writing stories for the *New Yorker* magazine and hoping that one day he would be able to write a novel. He was an artist, but he liked to keep up appearances. In the morning he got dressed in a business suit from Brooks Brothers with a rep tie and felt hat with a grosgrain band and rode down in our building elevator with all the other men dressed the same way on their way to work. They got off at the first floor and left the building through the lobby on their way to Wall Street and midtown.

My father crossed the lobby and walked down the back stairs to the basement, where he wrote all day in a windowless storage room in his boxer shorts, with his good suit carefully hung against the wall. The short stories he wrote in that small room were the beginnings of his masterful portraits of the city and the suburbs. "They seem to be stories of a long-lost world when the city of New York was still filled with river light, when you heard the Benny Goodman quartets from a radio in the corner stationery store, and when almost everybody wore a hat," he wrote about them decades later.

Unfortunately for me and my already full-blown love affair with Central Park, my parents had dreams that were too big for our rented two-bedroom apartment so close to the Queensborough Bridge that traffic noise was a constant part of our lives. They wanted more children and a family car. They longed for the postwar American chimera: a house with a white-picket fence. My brother Ben was born; my father bought a brown Dodge, which we all stroked and admired as if it was a new pet. Central Park with all its glories wasn't enough for my parents, and they didn't think it was enough for their children. They wanted a place in the "real" country, and this desire, the desire to migrate from the magical city to the endless driving and tidy little lawns of suburbia, seemed to animate their friends as well.

I was the lone dissenter. I did not want to go. I loved my urban school with its fenced-in playground perched above the East River Drive. I loved being able to go out by myself to the Boots Pharmacy on the corner, although later I learned that one of my parents always secretly followed me. Most of all I loved Central Park. In the summer we walked over to Bethesda Fountain to cool off. In the winter when the city air smelled of snow, we shouldered our skis—splintery slats of wood with huge coiling bindings—and slid shrieking with joy down the Seventy-ninth Street hill.

When we went to visit my parents' friends who had already made the move to Westchester or New Jersey, the so-called idyll of suburbia seemed a shabby comedown from

Central Park. Why would I want to swim in someone's muddy pond crawling with leeches when I could perch myself on a marble basin and cool myself with splashing clear water, topping it off with a lemonade from the cart on Fifth Avenue? Why would I want to scrape around the rough, dangerous ice of a country lake when I could glide around the smooth ice at the Wollman Rink and pause for a hot chocolate when my toes and fingers got too cold? Were these people crazy?

My family did move to the country, to a woodsy hamlet in Westchester on the Hudson River. We had lawns and woods to roam in and a wonderful big dog, but as soon as I was old enough to take the train back in to New York I did so at every opportunity. On many of these trips I wandered disconsolately around Central Park missing my old urban life. One of my haunts was the Frick Museum, where I would sit glumly on a bench in the inner courtyard until it was time to walk back down to Grand Central Terminal and take the train home for our suburban family dinner. The landscape paintings in the museum with their incandescent light—the Constables, the Turners—were more than enough country for me.

Later in my life I heard Andy Warhol say that it was better to live in the city than the country because in the city he could find a little bit of country, but in the country there was no little bit of city. He was so right! I could wander all I wanted in the suburban woods and try to be interested in the skunk cabbage that bloomed in the spring and the interesting patterns made by rotting logs next to a brook and the jelly blobs of frog's eggs in the pond, but none of it held a candle to the magnificent variety of the Conservatory Garden or even the rolling land around Cleopatra's Needle. I knew what Andy Warhol meant the moment I heard him say it, because for most of my life, Central Park has been my little bit of country.

Years later, I raised my own children in Central Park, where the wonderful urban public spaces are more fabulous than even the most luxurious rural private spaces. Raised as city kids—I vowed to let them grow up in the city and never, ever transplant them to the country—my son and daughter clambered over bronzes of bears and Alice in Wonderland in the winter and splashed in fanciful playground fountains in the summer, while their country friends played on mail-order swing sets and in plastic kiddy pools. Country children may have had ponies, but my kids had the delicious Carousel with its honky-tonk music and bright stallions. As a wheezy rendition of "Georgy Girl" piped over us, we whirled around in a state of bliss. Suburban children had fancy art classes; my children had the Metropolitan Museum of Art.

Although I have lived in many other places, I have always come back to New York City and to the Upper East Side. It's a wealthy neighborhood, but that isn't why I am here a few blocks from where I went to kindergarten. What makes it a rich place for anyone of any income is Central Park. As I grew up and married and my children grew up, the park continued to be my refuge for long walks and my weekend house, my family skating rink, my tennis court, my picnic spot, my dog run, and my gym. Every morning for years, in the heat of summer and the ice of winter, I headed for the running track around the Reservoir. Once I even saw Jacqueline Onassis on the track, which is now named after her. Anthony Quinn was another regular; he had a cab bring him over from his apartment on East End Avenue and wait parked on the bridle path while he ran around the track.

I have depended on Central Park for its usefulness, but its incidental beauty has often taken my breath away. I may look up from catching the flash of a scarlet tanager out of the corner of my eye, a tanager perched in the high branches of one of the huge cherry trees on the West Side, and my eyes hit the shimmering towers of midtown—the Plaza Hotel and the General Motors Building floating just above the Sheep Meadow. Sometimes while drifting in a creaky old rowboat rented for a trip on the Lake, I follow a flock of fuzzy ducklings just a stone's throw from the blaring horns of Columbus Circle.

It's the collision of man and nature, the collaboration of the human and the divine that makes the most poignant landscape: the terracing of an Italian hillside, a garden trellis, the lighthouses off the rocky New England coast. An ocean view is lovely but often monotonous, until a few boats appear. The sweep of green woods and mountain valleys in New Hampshire in the summer are catapulted into beauty by white church spires rising above the green. Central Park is one of the most delicious of these collisions of man and nature. Here the most intense city in the world is forcefully interrupted by some of the most glorious corridors of trees and abundant gardens in the United States.

My children are both in their twenties now, and we have two seasonal Central Park traditions these days—traditions which sometimes bring them back to New York from the cities where they live, New Orleans and Washington, D.C. For the past fifteen years, on New Year's Eve we have gone to Central Park for the glorious fireworks that go off at the start of the New Year, and the display of lighthearted human fortitude that is the traditional midnight run. Sometimes we run too, registering and collecting a T-shirt. Sometimes we just watch. Thousands of runners, many dressed in costume, many with dogs dressed to run in matching costumes, appear on the roadway above Bethesda Fountain to run around the park under the fireworks in the icy winter dark. It's freezing cold, but it's the best party of the night. After the run there is dancing in front of the Naumburg Bandshell until all hours of the morning.

Our summer tradition happens on or around my birthday at the end of July. Summers in New York City are blisteringly hot, but as the day cools down we head for Central Park and walk past the sailboat pond to the Loeb Boathouse on the Lake. We have dinner in the fading evening light at the Boathouse Restaurant at the edge of the water, and we eat at a table where the deck ends a few inches above the shimmering surface of the water. Ducks glide by looking for a handout, and we oblige them. There are a few boats still out, and the gondola drifts away and under the closest bridge. Suddenly the ducks scatter and turtles begin to rise out of the water to scarf up our discarded rosemary panini. First small turtles arrive and then the bigger ones come. One night the surface of the water heaved and buckled, and a turtle as big as a small car, a mossy prehistoric apparition in the middle of the city, inhaled the biggest chunk of our bread and then disappeared into the depths.

I have to confess that in the real country, far from other people and the cozy hum of electric generators and the clatter of traffic, I am often frightened. The nights are impossibly dark, and the animal noises from the deep woods, where coyotes chase rabbits and owls pick off their prey, terrify me. Nature in the country is not so cute. I listen to something howling in the trees on the other side of a flimsy cottage wall, and I feel utterly defenseless. I long for the safety of the city, where nature is so beautifully and spectacularly kept on a leash. I long for Manhattan, where my door is locked at night and the noises are the comforting human noises of cars and crowds. I long for the natural wonderland that is wild enough to delight and tame enough to enjoy—the wonderland called Central Park.

DONALD KNOWLER
The Falconer of Central Park

I N   A   C I T Y where people can live sixty-three thousand
to a square mile, Central Park represents the great escape. The park may be one of the most trampled patches of
greenery on Earth, but it still means freedom, a place for
pleasure, a breathing space.

I discovered the park in the winter of 1982, and that first
memory stayed with me through the spring and summer
months, the time when most New Yorkers use the park and
probably think the park is at its best. But a dusting of snow
undulating over smooth rocks, oyster-gray ice on the ponds,
skaters, blue jays begging peanuts—Central Park, for me, is
a Christmas card. If Charles Dickens had lived in the New
World, he would have threaded a description of Central
Park into his Christmas and winter tales. Mr. Pickwick
would have fallen through the ice there. The architecture of
the park lends itself to Victorian romanticism, and perhaps

the park's designers had a snowfall in mind when they created glades between pin oaks and the towering, turreted
majesty of the Belvedere Castle.

But I had not come to Central Park to study its design
or to observe its people. I wanted an introduction to the
wildlife of North America, and I had been told in Britain
that, surprisingly, Central Park could even offer that.

Central Park is a backyard for three million New Yorkers,
and I soon discovered why the park is featured so heavily in
the city's literature and folklore. It is a place where many
New Yorkers first feel grass under their feet, first become
aware of a bird or squirrel, learn to walk, to ride a bike, to
ice-skate. I was wandering in its acres during those first
days in January to pull my thoughts together. I had come to
New York in search of something I could not define, to take
stock, to find, not a new beginning, but an adjustment of
course, another avenue. If there had been a constant in my
life, it had been a casual interest in wildlife, and now, for
reasons I do not know, I was paying more attention to birds
than anything else, drawing irresistible parallels between
them and the people using the park.

A newspaper reported there was a "straggler" from Europe in the park, and I thought wryly it was a reference to
me. I had arrived in New York at short notice, with little
preparation, from my native Britain. The European bird
was a tufted duck, a very rare bird for North America, and
I was eager to see it because I remembered it as a familiar
sight in London during my childhood. My London has its
Hyde Park, Paris its Bois de Boulogne, but they do not bring

mankind and wildlife together. Wild creatures and humans there do not depend on parks for sustenance and sanity in the same way as New Yorkers do their park.

Central Park is interesting, too, because it is situated on a major migration route and is a staging point for many thousands of birds each spring and fall, besides providing shelter for wintering species. In the entire British Isles, it is difficult to see three hundred species of birds in a year; in Central Park a third of that number can be seen in a single day in May. I feared now, after discovering Central Park, I would return to London to find that city's premier open space as tame and predictable as its neatly manicured landscape.

I saw all the galleries and museums in my first few months in New York and found them an anticlimax. I thought they were overshadowed by a bigger and more glorious work of art, born of New York's sweat and ingenuity and not imported from Egypt, India, or Greece. The masterpiece is Central Park, and the fact that silt from its eroding surface clogs drains on the Museum Mile says much for the city's priorities and values, although a Central Park renaissance has begun in earnest to correct some of the devastation wrought when New York's financial problems reduced maintenance sharply.

Central Park is probably the most closely watched and monitored 843 acres on Earth. The debate among nature lovers about what is good for the park is only one aspect of a larger, continuing negotiation between all interested parties and the park authorities. The parties range from roller skaters to model-sailboat enthusiasts, to botanists and birders, to cyclists and joggers. They all want to extract the maximum benefit for themselves, and somewhere there must be a compromise, although the birders, in the main, maintain that nature has been compromised enough in the park, in the city, in the state, and in the country.

Central Park was undoubtedly designed with people in mind, but if its creators, Frederick Law Olmsted and Calvert Vaux, were alive today, they might also view the park as a microcosm of the global environmental crisis. They might agree with the birders who see the park as a symbolic last battleground on which man and his natural environment must settle their differences and reach an accommodation with each other that ensures the survival of both.

A KESTREL STOOD GUARD OVER THE LOCH in Central Park. From its perch in an elm, the small falcon many Americans know better as a sparrow hawk could see along the untidy streets of Harlem to the north. The Reservoir lay to the south, with the skyscrapers of Fifty-ninth Street and beyond half lost in the mist. A gentle rain and low pewter cloud blurred the gauntness of the trees. But the kestrel's vision was on the mark. About two hundred yards away he saw a chickadee working its way up the Loch, prizing sleeping bugs from the bark of oaks.

The kestrel, the drizzle giving a spiked appearance to his rufous plumage, eyed his prey carefully as the chickadee fluttered closer. The kestrel tilted forward on the twig high in the tree, arched his wings, and quietly, without a flap, started to swoop. Within seconds his wings were thrown back to act as a brake, and he hit the tiny chickadee with a smack. The blow carried the kestrel and the chickadee down toward the ground before the kestrel gained control again, with the screaming chickadee in his talons. Slow, powerful flaps were employed now as the kestrel and the chickadee rose through the gap in the branches. The other chickadees in the Loch had fallen silent, and the bird of prey, out in the clear sky, slowly lowered his head. With his precise, hooked beak, he bit into the neck of the chickadee, severing its vertebrae.

It was January 1, and in the Loch a clear stream tumbled over two waterfalls between oaks, elms, and red maples. Only the rising wail of a police-car siren and the rumble of subway trains under Central Park West fixed a time in history. And where once the American Indian and then the European trapper tiptoed in pursuit of deer, the mugger and the wildlife enthusiast tiptoed now.

THE PRESENCE OF THE KESTREL, and the rain, had washed all signs of life from the Loch. I tramped the stream where blue jays bathe in winter and cottontail rabbits come to drink in spring, and climbed above a waterfall near the west section of the park's circular drive. A bedraggled gray squirrel shook rain from its back and scampered over the roots of an oak on the far side of the road.

Someone was following me, but I did not see who. I headed for the Reservoir to the south in the hope of seeing something unusual or unexpected on the sheet of water, some rare species of gull or duck, knowing that at least the familiar wintering ducks would be there. Sure enough, a flotilla of three hundred lesser scaups was spread out along-side the west wall of the Reservoir, with a smattering of canvasbacks and ruddy ducks among them. The three spe-cies of duck, which had traveled thousands of miles to gather here in the very center of New York City, were es-caping from the biting winter that had gripped their breed-ing grounds to the north.

I had an uneasy feeling I was not alone. I glanced behind me. No one there. Central Park, the most popular and demo-cratic space in New York City, had become my best friend in the few lonely months I had lived in Manhattan, and I shrugged off warnings of its dangers. It held no menace, but neither did the streets of the city—then. I had yet to develop the New Yorker's instinct for survival—the "smarts."

As rain spotted the water, the blue, glossy heads of the male scaups were tucked into the fluffy gray feathers of their backs. The canvasbacks also slept, but some of the ruddy ducks chose to dive, scraping algae and other plant life from the bed of the Reservoir.

My eyes pressed into binoculars, and my body pushed against the wire mesh of the Reservoir fence, I did not no-tice my own predators. I felt something sharp between my shoulder blades, and I turned wildly, like the chickadee when it realized the kestrel was upon it. A man stood with a knife. "Give," he said nervously, a sodden felt hat hiding his face. He was joined by another man, who showed me the central spine of an umbrella, sharp and jagged where it had been snapped in two. I looked about me without mov-ing my head, fearing the slightest movement, the slightest twitch, would signal resistance and get me stabbed. There was no one else in sight, no rescuer. There was no point in delaying in parting with my wallet, so I held it out, and the mugger wearing the felt hat snatched it and ran.

It was my only dangerous moment, but an awareness of the park's potential for menace stayed with me during the entire year I spent exploring the park. I was the first of three bird-watchers mugged during 1982.

ON THE YEAR'S SECOND DAY, I was standing against the Reservoir fence, a little warier now. The scaups were in the same pose and place as the day before. A male, blinking, raised his head momentarily. A canvasback, his red eye standing out against the rusty color of his head, gave a sleeping female a passing glance as a gust of wind caught him and pushed him to the edge of the Reservoir. Quickly, he paddled back to join the flock. The tufted duck did not appear, but I was not particularly concerned I had missed the species. If the bird had been seen once during the winter, there was a good chance it would return, probably from feeding forays to the East and Hudson rivers.

On the third day, a freezing wind was blowing off the Reservoir from the north, and I wrapped a scarf tight around my face as I walked the water's southern rim, to the west side where the ducks had been all winter. In front of me, pushing into the Reservoir fence so it bulged around him, was a white-haired man, wrapped in concentration and heavy winter coat. Pointed woolen hat and conical beard, a gnome of a man. He held binoculars to a weathered face, and for a good fifteen minutes he did not move. I walked by twice, attempting to make conversation, but the birder either did not hear me or was not interested in talking. Finally, and loudly, I uttered the birder's identification call, "Anything around?"

The gnome, his white beard showing yellow nicotine stains, mumbled that there was a female ring-necked duck to the north, at the top end of the Reservoir a quarter of a mile away. I got the impression he did not want to be disturbed, because not once did he lower his binoculars.

"I suppose the report of the tufted duck was just wishful thinking," I said, proceeding to stroll north.

"No, I think I'm looking at a female," he said, lowering his binoculars now to rest his eyes. I felt a little disappointed that it was only the dull, brown female and not the striking black-and-white male. "See," said the birder, and in celebration of finding the bird he pulled an untipped cigarette from deep inside his coat. He then pointed to the raft of five hundred male and female scaups and declared there was a second tufted duck among them somewhere, and he would find it. I stayed, too, feet frozen and talking of birds.

The birder's name was Lambert Pohner. For forty years, he had been coming to the park, and he reckoned he had seen more than two hundred species there but had stopped counting. He said if I had an hour to spare he would show me a book in which the park's regular birders listed the species they had seen. Walking across the Great Lawn, past hooded figures out jogging in the dim light and watching for late afternoon muggers, Lambert Pohner told me more about the birds of the park, and the animals, reptiles, and insects. He mentioned the pair of raccoons living under the rotting, disused boats at the Loeb Boathouse; the bullfrog, turtles, and carp in the boating lake, the strutting killdeer that rest during migration on the Great Lawn.

The bird register was in a loose-leaf binder, chained to the counter of the boathouse cafeteria. The entry recording the tufted duck was signed the "mob." (I later learned this meant "many old birders.") Someone else claimed to have seen a bald eagle sailing over Broadway in December ("honestly, I did . . ."), and squeezed between the duck and eagle were details of a mugging. Incidents of robbery and descriptions of muggers were faithfully recorded along with the birds.

The hard-core Central Park birding fraternity—those who are on hand in even the worst weather—numbers about fifty. There is no "average" or stereotypical birder, although people who regard bird-watching as an eccentricity like to believe there is. Among birders I know of is a man who talks loudly because he spent his working life in the railroad switching yard, a viola player with the New York Philharmonic who has an ear for bird songs, and a used-car salesman who frequently warned me about "lemons," which I did not know grew in the park. Another birder is a retired policeman, and another, I am told, was a bank robber, now deceased.

The bank-robber story is a favorite when the birders are confined to Central Park's boathouse: It seems the bank robber carried a little black book in his back pocket in which he recorded his life list of birds spotted. He told other birders he was a writer, and for long periods he was not seen in the park. He had been traveling for research purposes, he said when he returned. Then one day another birder saw an item in a newspaper about a man shot dead while trying to rob a bank in San Francisco. The police, so the story goes, returned the robber's life list to the boathouse.

It is raining. The bank-robber story is finished, and now comes a second favorite: a tale about the policeman birder who, when he was wearing his uniform, was one of the most popular people in the park. Once, according to this story, the emperor of Japan paid a visit to Central Park, for reasons that are obscure now. But his visit coincided with the bird migration, and the policeman birder went on duty with his binoculars, commandeered a rowboat, and, from the center of the boating lake, spent the afternoon scanning willows for warblers. One of the top officers of the New York City force saw the policeman birder and later commended him for his "initiative." The officer thought the policeman was looking for snipers.

The first snow flurries of the winter, followed by freezing rain, arrived on January 9. The water lapping at the cemented stone sides of the Reservoir turned into ice coral as it gripped stems of grass and reeds. Next day the temperature dropped to well below freezing. Vast tracts of ice formed at the north end of the Reservoir, and hundreds of ducks had chosen to leave on a journey farther south to find ice-free wintering areas.

Most of the United States was coated with the coldest weather of the century. My hands froze through two pairs of gloves. Somewhere in my heavy boots I had lost my feet, and I could not believe New York could get colder than this. But it did the next day, the thermometer at the Central Park weather observatory reading only five degrees Fahrenheit. Mist rose from the rapidly freezing water of the Reservoir; air warmed by the sun formed "sea smoke" as it came into contact with the freezing water, the great swirls of moisture meandering in steamy streams. It was beautiful but so cold.

The front that had moved in from Russia via the Arctic was dubbed "the Siberian Express" by weathermen, and five days after its arrival the Reservoir had completely frozen over. Giant chunks of ice in different shades of gray formed in strata against the Reservoir wall, and a low, black cloud warned of snow. Six inches fell, and I was up early to look for raccoon tracks around the boathouse. For an hour I hunted, only to find furrows made by squirrels who were burrowing for food supplies hidden in fall. The squirrels bury more nuts and seeds than they will find and are an important tool in the process of reforestation. The food they do locate is invariably stolen by blue jays, once the cache has been revealed. The jays, not appreciating how deep the snow lay, were submerged momentarily as they pounced on acorns and beechnuts exposed by the squirrels. Emerging, they shook the snow off their beaks with rapid, indignant flicks of the head.

If there is an equivalent of a human mugger in the animal

world, I suppose it has to be the blue jay. But the blue jay stops short of outright violence. It is a hustler, a bully, but rarely a killer, and is usually the first bird to warn others of danger in the woods. The blue jay would be the type of mugger who takes your wallet but leaves you with enough money to take a taxi home, or lets you keep your laundry receipts. A newspaper in the first weeks of January had run a story about a Broadway mugger who gave back to an out-of-town couple their theater tickets. He would have been a blue-jay mugger.

The wind swirled snow in the zoo while a polar bear called Scandy paced up and down in his small cage, agitated. In the snow and cold, the bear looked one degree saner than he would appear in the high humidity of summer, when he seemed quite mad. A child leaned over the outer rail of the bear's cage, and Scandy rushed at the bars, banging his head so a smudge of red showed on the ivory of his fur. Later in the year Scandy killed a man who scaled several fences to get into his cage. The polar bear, protective of his space, had the haunted look of so many of the people beyond the bars, out there in a city where humans fight for every square inch of space and you can be stepped over dropping dead in the street. And where the lonely and frightened lock themselves voluntarily in their own cages and feel alone.

SEVENTEEN DAYS HAD passed since I had seen the kestrel take the chickadee, and he had now learned there were easy pickings around the sour gum in the Ramble, where bird-feed is suspended during the winter months. It was a convenient place for me to observe a bird of prey going about his brutal business, and, keeping myself concealed, I saw both him and his much larger mate many times after that.

In the area around the feeder tree, the birds were becoming incredibly tame. The cheekier titmice and chickadees were not alone in begging for food. A male cardinal came so close on an overhanging branch that I could have touched him. But, unlike the others, he refused to take a peanut from outstretched palm. He simply jerked his black chinned head downward, instructing me to throw the nut to the ground, but close to him so the blue jays would not steal it. I followed his instructions, and with a "cheep" that was barely audible, the cardinal dropped into the snow to retrieve the nut. Two females gave me the same instruction, and all the while the chickadees and titmice tried to attract my attention by dropping level with my head before flying back to an adjacent branch.

The bond between man and the wild creatures that share his immediate environment is cemented in that simple act of feeding a bird by hand. The birds, even if desperate for food, must be trusting and confident that this giant figure bearing gifts is also bearing goodwill. It is a thrilling, moving experience for the benefactor. The bird homes in so fast you flinch, thinking it will not stop and will career into you. Before you are fully aware of it, the bird is gripping your fingers with tiny, sharp claws. The chickadees usually grab the nut and fly off immediately, but their relatives, the titmice, with crests erect in curiosity, pause for a moment to look you in the face.

Two weeks after the arrival of the Siberian Express, a slight rise in temperature caused the ice on the Reservoir to thaw in places. But temperatures barely climbed above freezing point for the rest of January, and snow continued to coat the park. In the Ramble, squirrels begged for food after losing their hoards to the blue jays. They would stand on hind legs, front paws tucked into furry stomachs, and in the feeding area a squirrel accustomed to a daily handout came up to me and prodded my boots with its nose. It was while I fed the squirrel that the fabled yellow-bellied sapsucker came into view.

If the sapsucker did not exist, the people who satirize bird-watchers would invent it. The bird's quaint name is synonymous with stout boots and binoculars, with superenthusiasts who appear out of step with a fast-paced world beyond the park's boundaries. The sapsucker was the first I had seen, and I thought he deserved better than ridicule. The bird embodied a subtle beauty, yellow wash to his body and a splash of red on his black-and-white patterned head.

The species is easy to observe because it is not as active as other woodpeckers. Instead of darting from tree to tree, it prefers to stay put to drill neat lines of holes. As its name suggests, it will return later to drink the sap oozing from the holes and to eat insects attracted to it. This particular bird spent forty minutes drilling a pine, all the time sending flakes of bark and wood to the ground, like falling snow.

I watched an oiled canvasback that had probably landed in an oil slick on one of New York's bays. He looked in dreadful shape twenty-four hours after I had first seen him.

Forlornly, he paddled through the water, his plumage without its usual sheen. He struggled to climb out of the water, pushing his chest onto the ice, trying to cock up his left leg, then slipping and plunging backward into the water. After several attempts, he waddled ashore, a patch of oily, matted feathers visible. While in the water, the duck had tilted his body to try to preen himself, but he soon gave this up.

Canvasbacks, being estuarine ducks, spend much time out in New York City's bays, and they often fall victim to oil spills from coastal tankers. It was clear he was dying, and within two days he was dead. His body had been dragged about forty yards by gulls, and I watched a greater black-backed gull feeding on the carcass. The carelessness of someone handling oil meant the canvasback would not make it back to his breeding ground more than a thousand miles to the northwest.

The sun was warm, and I went looking for an owl that had been making visits to the park. On the frozen model-boat pond, a girl skated; a teenager in fawn beret and blue jersey and slacks, beautiful and willowy as she cut through the ice, twirling and jumping clear of the surface. Hans Christian Andersen looked on, ignoring a squirrel running across his open bronze book. Nearby a bag lady slouched on a green wooden bench. She was the first bag person I had seen in the park during the month, although evidence of their encampments could be seen in hidden corners of the woods. The bag lady, a frown distorting her tanned, hairy face, wore a quilted coat over bulging woolens to keep out the cold. Layers of socks forced their way out of holes in the sides of her sneakers. The woman, surrounded by a suitcase and three shopping bags, swore at the girl who was skating, but the skater did not look up.

I CLIMBED TO the Point, a rocky promontory nudging into the boating lake, and for once felt claustrophobic in the park. The sharp early-evening sunshine from over the East River cast the buildings all around in vertical lines of light and shadow, and this made them loom larger than they really were. The air was clear and winter-fresh, and this seemed to bring the buildings and their fine detail even closer; the newer skyscrapers like black-and-gold cigarette lights standing on a rough-hewn table of oak. The Point faces due south, and now I could see the park in relation to the city—a narrow, fertile strip resisting concrete and glass.

MARIE WINN
About Those Ducks, Holden

D EAR HOLDEN CAULFIELD,
I know it's probably too late and you don't give a
damn about such things anymore—you're probably in
some crummy retirement community in Florida or Arizona
or somewhere, for crying out loud. Here's how I figure it:
In 1945, when your author, J. D. Salinger, published the
first story about you in *Collier's* magazine, you were a junior
in high school. So you're probably getting Social Security
by now.

But all through *The Catcher in the Rye* you kept asking
a question, a really good question, and nobody ever gave
you an answer. It was pathetic. I mean, you really wanted
some information, and in chapter 12 all Horwitz the taxi
driver would say was "How the hell should I know?" No
wonder you ended up in a loony bin in the last chapter. I
hope I'm not giving away any secrets or anything, but

Catcher's been out for a long time and I guess most people know how it ends by now.

You remember your question, the one about the ducks in Central Park. You were worried about what happens to those ducks when all the lakes freeze over. You wondered whether some guy came in a truck and took them away to a zoo or something. It showed that you were a sensitive kid, Holden, it really did, your caring about the ducks and everything. I mean, most people just don't give a damn about the animals in the park and all.

Well, all these years I've kind of wondered about your question myself. But not very hard. Because things have changed since the 1940s or '50s when you were getting kicked out of that phony prep school and meeting old Sally Hayes under the clock at the Biltmore. Would you believe it, Holden, that clock isn't there anymore. They've taken down the whole damn hotel, for chrissake!

But that's not what I mean when I say that things have changed. I mean that it hasn't been so cold these winters.

I remember Central Park in the '40s and '50s. In those days it got really cold in January or February. Kids used to actually ice-skate on the old rowboat lake. Like me and my sister old Janet used to skate there all the time, and so did a lot of other people. Of course we didn't have much choice if we wanted to skate because they didn't have any skating rinks in the park in those days. There was only the rink at Rockefeller Center, and that one was too expensive. Besides, all the girls there had these little skating dresses with white fur at the hem and sleeves. I didn't have one.

In those days, I'm sorry to tell you, Holden, I didn't worry about the ducks like you did—I honestly never gave the ducks a single thought. I don't know what was wrong with me. Something, I guess, because I never got kicked out of school, either.

By the time I grew up and began to really care about ducks and stuff the winters stopped being so cold. I don't know why, exactly, maybe the greenhouse effect or whatever. But it's the truth. The lakes in Central Park hardly ever froze over during the last few decades, not solidly so you could skate on them, and not all over so anybody had to worry about the ducks.

But recently I've been thinking about you a lot, Holden. Really I have. Because this has been one unbelievably cold winter. I mean it's been really cold. All the lakes and even the Reservoir in Central Park have frozen solid. People are skating on the rowboat lake, for chrissake, and I haven't seen anybody do that for about five hundred years, not since I was a little girl. So your question began to really bother me.

And guess what, Holden? I actually found out what happens to the ducks in Central Park when everything freezes over. And I can tell you that nobody comes with a truck and takes them away to the zoo or anything.

My friend Bill DeGraphenreid figured it out. He's this nice dark-skinned guy with a big shock of white hair who feeds the ducks all year. I mean he really cares about the ducks and he brings them huge amounts of food all the time. And imagine this: he actually knows those ducks. I'm not kidding, it's absolutely amazing. There's this one female mallard he calls Missy, and there's all Missy's children—she had eight ducklings last spring—and there's Missy's sister—he calls her Missy, too—who was slightly crippled from getting tangled in fishing line. When he calls "Missy, Missy!" one of the Missys always comes.

Anyhow, when all the lakes froze this year Bill began to worry about the ducks. So he looked all over the park for them. Finally he found them. All of them. Hundreds of ducks, including Missy and Missy's sister. They were all in a secret place, just about the only place in all of Central Park that hadn't frozen over. Because there's an actual natural spring that runs into it, while all the other streams in the park turn on and off with a faucet, for chrissake.

So Bill's been going there just about every day with heaps of food for Missy I and Missy II and all the other ducks, even though the roads in the park have been horribly icy and besides, he has this painful foot condition, called bone spurs, that makes it hard to walk.

So Holden, I'm going to tell you how to find the secret place where the Central Park ducks go when all the lakes are frozen over. Do you know where Balcony Bridge is? It's this structure that is actually a part of the West Drive, somewhere around 77th Street. If you stand on its east side you get a fantastic view of the rowboat lake and the Central Park South and Fifth Avenue skylines. From its west side you're facing the Natural History Museum.

Well, all the ducks are down there under old Balcony Bridge, hundreds of ducks and nobody hardly notices them.

But if you stand there facing Fifth Avenue and throw down a lot of bread you'll see them all right. They'll all come out and push and shove and gobble up every crumb. You should come and do it, Holden. It'll make you so damn happy it'll just about kill you. It really will.

BILL BUFORD
Lions and Tigers and Bears

S O I T H O U G H T I'd spend the night in Central Park, and, having stuffed my small rucksack with a sleeping bag, a big bottle of mineral water, a map, and a toothbrush, I arrived one heavy, muggy Friday evening in July to do just that: to walk around until I got so tired that I'd curl up under a tree and drop off to a peaceful, outdoorsy sleep. Of course, anybody who knows anything about New York knows the city's essential platitude—that you don't wander around Central Park at night—and in that, needless to say, was the appeal: it was the thing you don't do. And, from what I can tell, it has always been the thing you don't do, ever since the Park's founding commissioners, nearly a hundred and fifty years ago, decided that the place should be closed at night—a decision heartily endorsed by its coarchitect Frederick Law Olmsted, who said that once the Park was dark he'd "answer for no man's safety in it from bullies, garroters, or highway robbers." At the time, the commissioners were re-covering from one of the Park's first fatalities: the result of a downtown lad's overturning his two-wheeler and snapping his neck in a brandy-inspired carriage race down the Mall. Most felons then were reckless carriage drivers. In modern times, they're distinctly more menacing, as Ogden Nash ob-served in 1961.

> *If you should happen after dark*
> *To find yourself in Central Park,*
> *Ignore the paths that beckon you*
> *And hurry, hurry to the zoo,*
> *And creep into the tiger's lair.*
> *Frankly, you'll be safer there.*

Even now, when every Park official, city administrator, and police officer tells us (correctly) that the Park is safe during the day, they all agree in this: only a fool goes there at night. Or a purse snatcher, loon, prostitute, drug dealer, homophobic gay basher, murderer—not to mention bully, garroter, highway robber.

I arrived at nine-fifteen and made for the only nocturnal spot I knew: the Delacorte Theatre. Tonight's show was *The Taming of the Shrew.* "Bonny Kate," Petruchio was saying, "she is my goods, my chattel . . . my horse, my ox, my ass, my any thing." Lights out, applause, and the audience began exiting through the tunnels at the bottom of the bleachers. So far, so normal, and this could have been an outdoor summer-stock Shakespeare production anywhere in America, except in one respect: a police car had pulled up just as Petruchio began his soliloquy and was now parked conspicuously in view, its roof light slowly rotating. The police were there to reassure the audience that it was being protected; the rotating red light was like a campfire in the wild, warning what's out there to stay away.

The Park has had its own police precinct since the end of the nineteenth century, and it is now staffed with what Police Commissioner Howard Safir, himself an evening-roller-blading Park enthusiast, describes as "people persons"—well-spoken, well-mannered policemen whose first task is to make visitors feel happy. And, on any normal visit, I, like anyone else, would actually be very happy to see one of the men in blue. But not tonight. It's against the law to spend the night in the Park, and at around eleven o'clock the police start their "sweep"—crisscrossing the place on foot and in unmarked cars, scooters, little three-wheeled vans, and helicopters.

During my first hour or so, I wandered around the Delacorte, reassured by the lights, the laughter, the lines of Shakespeare that drifted out into the summer night. I was feeling a certain exhilaration, the euphoria that comes from doing the thing you're not meant to be doing, climbing the steps of Belvedere Castle all alone, peeking through the windows of the Henry Luce Nature Observatory, identifying the herbs in the Shakespeare Garden, seeing no one, when, after turning this way and that, I was on a winding trail in impenetrable foliage, and, within minutes, I was lost.

There was a light ahead, and as I rounded the corner I

came upon five men, all wearing white tank-top T-shirts, huddled around a bench. I walked past, avoiding eye contact, and turned down a path, a narrow one, black dark, going down a hill, getting darker, very dark. Is this a good idea? I asked myself, when, as if on cue, I heard a great shaking of the bushes beside me and froze. Animal? Mugger? Whatever I was hearing would surely stop making that noise, I thought. But it didn't. How can this be? I'm in the Park less than an hour and already I'm lost, on an unlighted path, facing an unknown thing shaking threateningly in the bushes. It was no small thing moving around in there, and, what's more, it was moving in my direction, and I thought, Shit! What *am* I doing here? And I bolted, not running, exactly, but no longer strolling—and certainly not looking back—turning left, turning right, all sense of direction obliterated, the crashing continuing behind me, louder even, *left*, another man in a tank-top T-shirt, *right*, another man, when I finally realized where I was—in the Ramble, stupid, where I'd been only once before (and got lost)—as I turned left again, and there was a lake, and the skyline of Central Park South, the Essex House Hotel, and the reassuring sign for A&E's *Biography*, announcing the temperature (eighty-two degrees), the time (ten-fifteen), and tonight's *Biography* special (William Shatner). I stopped. I breathed. Relax, I told myself. It's only darkness.

About fifteen feet into the lake, there was a large boulder, with a heap of branches leading to it. I tiptoed across and sat, enjoying the picture of the city again, the very reassuring city. I looked around. There was a warm breeze, and heavy clouds overhead, but it was still hot, and I was sweating. Far out in the lake, there was a light—someone rowing a boat, a lantern suspended above the stern. I got my bearings—the twin towers of the San Remo in view, a penthouse all lit up, a party. I was on the West Side, around Seventy-seventh. People use the cross streets, imaginatively projecting them across the Park, like latitude lines, as a way of imposing a New York grid on this bit of New York gridlessness. The far side of the lake must be near Strawberry Fields, around Seventy-second. Just where that boat was now, I realized, was where, two years ago, the police had found the body of Michael McMorrow, a forty-four-year-old man (my age), who was stabbed thirty-four times by a fifteen-year-old. It was possible, the thought occurred to me, to chart my progress through the Park via its recent murders (I entered at East Seventy-second, where, two months ago, the police found the body of a publishing executive, inexplicably felled, the headphones of his Walkman still clamped to his ears, and later, as I headed for the Reservoir . . .), but no, this didn't seem like a fruitful way of organizing the evening. Even so, the menacing Central Park crime mystique lingered: the idea that here anything is possible. You enter the Park, you have sex in the bushes with a stranger, you leave. No memory, no trace. You find someone all alone, you rob him, you disappear. Unseen transgressions. After McMorrow was killed, he was disemboweled, his intestines ripped out so that his body would sink when rolled into the lake—a detail that I've compulsively reviewed in my mind since I first heard it. And then his killers, with time on their hands and no witnesses, just went home. Another feature of a Central Park crime: no one knows you're here.

One of the first events in the Park took place 140 years ago almost to the day: a band concert. The concert, pointedly, was held on a Saturday, still a working day, because the concert, like much of the Park then, was designed to keep the city's rougher elements out. The Park at night must have seemed luxurious and secluded—a giant evening garden party. There were no other entertainments. No rides, no playgrounds, no vendors. The Park was to be strolled through, enjoyed as an aesthetic experience, like a walk inside a painting. George Templeton Strong, the indefatigable diarist, was an early Park user. On his first visit, on June 11, 1859, the place was a desolate landscape of mounds of compost and lakes without water. But even at that stage Strong recognized that the architects were building two different parks at once. One was the Romantic park, which included the Ramble, the thirty-seven-acre, carefully "designed" wilderness, wild nature re-created in the middle of the city, *rus in urbe*, an English notion—nature as surprising and unpredictable. The other, the southern end of the Park, was more French: ordered, and characterized by straight lines. Strong was unhappy with the straight lines and could see that once the stunted elms were fully grown ("by A.D. 1950," he wrote) the place would look distinctly "Versailles-y." But by 1860 this section was tremendously popular, and paintings show a traffic jam of fancy carriages, all proceeding the wrong way up Fifth Avenue—"a broad torrent of vehicular gentility wherein profits shoddy and of petroleum were largely represented," Strong wrote in disgust.

I climbed back down from the rock. In the distance, I spotted a couple approaching. An uncomfortable thing: someone else in the Park. Your first thought is: nutcase? But then I noticed, even from a hundred feet, that the couple was panicking: the man was pulling the woman to the other side of him, so that he would be between her and me when we passed. The woman stopped, and the man jerked her forward authoritatively, and there was a muted exchange. I was surprised by how expressive their fear was—even in the way they were moving. As they got closer, I could see that he was tall and skinny, wearing a plaid shirt and black horn-rimmed glasses; she was blonde, and looked determinedly at the ground, her face rigid. Both of them were now walking fast and stiffly. When they were within a few feet of me, he reached out and grabbed her arm. I couldn't resist: just as we were about to pass each other, I addressed them, forth-rightly: "Hello, good people!" I said. "And how are you on this fine summer evening?" At first, silence, and then the woman started shrieking uncontrollably—"Oh, my God! Oh, my God!"—and they hurried away.

This was an interesting discovery. One of the most fright-ening things in the Park at night was a man on his own. One of the most frightening things tonight was me. I was emboldened by the realization, newly confident: I was no longer afraid; I was frightening. Another man approached, big and fat, wearing only shorts, with blubbery tits hanging over his swollen belly. Ah, well, I thought, someone who really is insane. No matter. I greeted him. He was very friendly. He had an aluminum container of food, and he was eating as he walked. He offered me some.

"What is it?" I asked.

"Pasta," he said. "Mmm, mmm. Would you like a bite?"

"No, thanks," I said. "I've eaten."

"You sure?" he said. "I got plenty."

"No, really," I said. "That's very kind, but I couldn't."

Not everyone likes the Park, but just about everyone feels he should. This was at the heart of Henry James's otherwise impressively incomprehensible observations when he visited the Park, in 1904. The Park, in James's eyes, was a failure. All the fake nature stuff, got up to be so many wild scenes, was not unlike "the effect of those old quaint prints which give in a single view the classic, gothic and other architectural wonders of the world." The Park was too narrow, and too short, and was overwhelmed by an obligation to "do." The most remarkable thing about it was simply that it existed, and any person who didn't, as James put it, "keep patting the Park on the back" was guilty of being seen as a social ingrate. By then, the Park's founders had died, and the Park, no longer the domain of the privileged, had been taken over by immigrants—a "polyglot Hebraic crowd of pedestrians," in James's inelegantly revealing phrase. In fact, between James's visit and the nineteen-thirties, the Park might well have been at its most popular, visited by more people than today, when current estimates put the number of visitors somewhere between ten and twenty million a year. The Park in fact was being destroyed by overuse, until 1934, when the legendary Robert Moses, genius urban impresario and civic fascist, was appointed parks commissioner. Moses was responsible for the third design element in the Park—neither English nor French, neither Romantic nor classical, but efficient, purposeful, and unapologetically American. All that arty pretend-you're-in-a-painting-of-the-Hudson-River-School: he had no time for it. He wanted baseball diamonds, shuffleboard, volleyball, and swimming pools. He closed the Casino—originally the tea salon of the Park's other architect, Calvert Vaux, but by the nineteen-thirties a dubious if highly charismatic speakeasy of jazz, celebrities, and corrupt glamour—and replaced it, characteristically, with a playground. Even the Ramble became a target: Moses tried to chop it down and install a fourteen-acre senior citizens' recreation center. He was blocked by the protesting bird-watchers—one of the few times Moses was stopped. The irony was that by the end of the Moses era the Park—no longer a piece of nature but a piece of property, a venue for recreation, not conservation—was dangerous.

In my new confidence I set out for the northern end of the Park. Near the reservoir, a gang of kids on bicycles zoomed across the Eighty-fifth Street Transverse, hooting with a sense of ominous power. A little later, there was another gang, this one on foot—about a dozen black kids, moving eastward, just by the running track. I kept my head down and picked up my pace, but my mind involuntarily called up the memory of the 1989 "wilding" incident, in which a young investment banker was beaten and sexually assaulted by a group of kids on a rampage.

Around Ninety-fifth Street, I found a bench and stopped. I had taken one of the trails that run alongside the Park's West Drive, and the more northern apartments of Central Park West were in view. I sat as residents prepared for bed: someone watching television, a woman doing yoga, a man stepping into the shower. Who needs curtains when it's only the Park outside your window? Below me was the city, the top of the Empire State Building peeking over the skyline. George Templeton Strong discovered the beauty of Central Park at night on July 30, 1869, on a "starlit drive" with his wife. But what Strong saw was different from what I was looking at. The Park was darker then than now, genuinely empty, and something much closer to Olmsted's nature in the seeming wild. And, of course, you could see the stars. Tonight, even if it weren't clouding over, there'd be no stars. Too much glare. The Park is now framed, enveloped even, by the city in a way that Olmsted never imagined, but there was no escaping the recognition that this city—contrived, man-made, glaringly obtrusive, consuming wasteful and staggering quantities of electricity and water and energy— was very beautiful. I'm not sure why it should be so beautiful; I don't have the vocabulary to describe its appeal. But there it was: the city at night, viewed from what was meant to be an escape from it, shimmering.

Olmsted's son, also a landscape architect, was offended by the tall buildings that had begun crowding round his father's achievement. It was ruinous, the son said, "ugly, restless, and distressing," and there was talk of limiting the height of what greedy real estate developers could build. Young Olmsted did not understand the romance of what was taking form.

A policeman appeared. It was after midnight, and I thought that my visit was now terminated. But he could see that I was enjoying the view, so he found a bench not far away. He had a shaved head and a mild manner. He said nothing and took in the view himself. And that was what we did, sitting together, separated by twenty or thirty feet, in silence, for ten minutes, saying nothing, until finally I felt I could get up, and said good night, and resumed my journey.

I walked around the Harlem Meer, busy even at one in the morning—couples on benches, young men hunched over their girlfriends like question marks. From the hill of Fort Clinton, where the British drove Washington's troops north and took temporary possession of Manhattan, I watched a slow seduction. I walked and walked. Around one-thirty, I entered the North Woods, and made my way down to what my map would later tell me was a stream called the Loch. The stream was loud, sounding more like a river than a stream. And for the first time that night the city disappeared: no buildings, no lights, no sirens.

I was tired. I had been walking for a long time. I wanted to unroll my sleeping bag, out of view of the police, and fall asleep. I was looking forward to dawn and being awakened by birds.

I made my way down a ravine. A dirt trail appeared on

my left. This looked promising. I followed it, and it wound its way down to the stream. I looked back: I couldn't see the trail; it was blocked by trees. This was good. Secluded. I walked on. It flattened out and I could put a sleeping bag here. This was good, too. Yes: good. There were fireflies, even at this hour, and the place was so dark and so densely shrouded by the trees overhead that the light of the fireflies was hugely magnified; their abdomens pulsed like great yellow flashlights. There was also a smell: a dampness, a kind of rotting fecundity. And the stream was very loud: this was the sound of nature, true, but it was all a bit too incongruous. Olmsted or not, I knew I was in Harlem.

I spotted a white article on the ground. I stared at it for a while before walking over to pick it up. It was a woman's blouse. Of course. A woman had simply left it behind. Fifty yards from here, a Brazilian jogger was killed—the murderer never found. (A week later, a woman would be murdered nearby, at the Blockhouse, at this very hour, her screams ignored by a resident who heard them. When I returned here, at midnight two nights after that killing, I, too, would hear a woman's screams—spooky, bleating screams, which I then reported to a policeman, startling him in the dark where I tracked him down.)

I eventually rolled out my sleeping bag atop a little rise beside the bridle path by the North Meadow, and then I sat, cross-legged, and asked myself questions: Why did I bring a little airline tube of toothpaste but no flashlight? Why didn't I bring a cell phone? Wouldn't a can of Mace have been prudent? I crawled inside my bag and closed my eyes. And then: *snap!* A tremendous cracking sound. I froze, then quickly whipped round to have a look: nothing. A forest is always full of noises. How did I manage to camp out as a kid? Finally, I fell asleep.

I know I fell asleep because I was awake again. Another branch snapping, but this sound was different—as if I could hear the tissue of the wood tearing. My eyes still closed, I was motionless. Another branch, and then a rustling of leaves. No doubt: someone was there. I could tell I was being stared at; I could feel the staring. I heard breathing.

I opened my eyes and was astonished by what I saw. I was surrounded by—what? Something. There were three of them, all within arm's reach. They looked very big. At first I didn't know what they were, except that they were animals. The only animal I'd seen in the Park was a rat. These were not rats—that was my first thought. Actually, that was my second thought; my first was: This is not the police. Maybe they were bears, small ones. Then I realized; they were—what do you call them? Those animals that Daniel Boone made his hat out of.

They weren't moving; I wasn't moving. They just stared, brown eyes looking blankly into my own. They were obviously very perplexed to find me here. Suddenly, I was very perplexed to find me here, too. "Imagine this," one of them seemed to be saying. "A grown man sleeping out in Central Park!"

"Obviously, not from New York."

"Hi, guys," I muttered. I said this very softly.

My voice startled them and they scurried up the tree in

front of me. But only ten feet up. Then they stopped and resumed staring. And then, very slowly, they inched a little farther up. What should I do? If I ignored them and fell asleep, I faced the prospect of their coming down again. On the other hand, why would I want to frighten them? Besides, what if I frightened them and they *didn't* leave? After all, I was now in their way. They inched a little farther. They were about forty feet up, directly above me now, and the tree was swaying slightly with their weight.

It was starting to drizzle. I heard a helicopter, its searchlight crisscrossing the bridle path only ten feet away. So maybe there were bad guys.

I looked back at the raccoons. "Are there bad guys here?" I asked them. It was stupid to speak. My voice startled them and, directly overhead, one of them started peeing. And then, nature finding herself unable to resist, it started to pour.

But not for long. The rain stopped. The raccoons stared. And I fell asleep. I know I fell asleep because the next thing I heard was birds. A natural, naturally beautiful sound.

BROOKS HANSEN
Beastie

He's the only one that they let see them;
they're the only ones that he lets see—
they're not alone,
there's flesh and bone,
there's pointy ears, and fingernails and teeth.

W E'VE COME TO make a purchase!" announced
Mrs. Guildenweiser, holding Phillip's mother's
voucher high above her head as they all three entered—
first Lara (her black poodle), then Mrs. Guildenweiser, then
Phillip. Still, all he needed was to hear the familiar clang and
jingle of the door closing behind them to know that she was
right: If anything could take his mind off what had been happening the last few days, it was Mr. DiFrancini's soldier shop.

No one else was there—other than Mr. DiFrancini, of
course, who was sitting behind the counter in back, quietly

leafing through a collector's book. Phillip liked Mr. DiFrancini. He always wore vests, and even though his great bald forehead and equally large round chin made his head look like a giant peanut, there was something very dignified about him. Lara was prancing around the space now, thwacking the glass cabinets with her tail, but Mr. DiFrancini barely glanced up. He rarely said a word, in fact, and only made eye contact when you actually bought something, which Phillip appreciated, because it meant you never felt rushed at Mr. DiFrancini's. You hardly felt noticed.

The centerpiece had changed since the last time Phillip was here. The Indian hunting the buffalo had been moved over to the corner, and in its place was a bronze whaling boat, smashing against a bronze wave, and a harpooner standing, ready to throw. Phillip could have stared at it for hours, but he didn't tempt himself. As Mrs. Guildenweiser made her way around to Mr. DiFrancini to present the voucher and discuss terms, Phillip turned his attention to the glass cases that lined the walls and housed what he judged to be the far more crucial (and affordable) part of Mr. DiFrancini's enterprise: the miniature soldiers.

Mr. DiFrancini only sold the highest quality, never the plastic molded kind. His were hand-painted and made of lead and pewter, planted on sturdy metal bases. Phillip had three—a knight on horseback and two Civil War infantrymen—which stood out from the rest of his collection like jewels among stones. He already knew which piece he wanted today, but he still made his round as usual, starting with the first case on the right-hand side, which was filled entirely with knights in armor, knights on horseback, knights with plumed helmets and working visors and chain mail vests and flags with griffins.

The next case over was French foreign legion, with kerchiefs on their caps. Then Arabs and Arabian horses, and camels; then revolutionary soldiers, redcoats and militiamen, and Indians and the French as well. There were World War I soldiers, and World War II, down on their stomachs and crawling, and kneeling, and charging. There were heavy tanks and planes.

But Phillip's favorite by far were the Civil War soldiers. Mr. DiFrancini had two cases for them—blues and the grays alike—infantrymen and cavalry, lieutenants and generals, as well as several tents and cannon. Phillip would have taken any of them happily, but the one that he was most interested in stood just beyond a regiment of Zouaves: a Union Trooper on his horse. He wore a blue double-breasted shirt with gold buttons, a gold neckerchief, two chevrons, and a small-visored cap. He had a very thick mustache, and his eyes were trained on the horizon in a squint. His pants were gray, boots black. He had a sword, a sheath, a pistol, and a tobacco pouch. His horse was in full gallop, tail whipping behind him like a flag.

"Is that your choice?" came a voice from behind, Mr. DiFrancini's, as always in a much kinder and calmer tone than Phillip expected.

Phillip nodded, and Mr. DiFrancini started over, pulling a key from the reel on his belt. He unlocked the glass case and slid the pane to the side. "The Trooper, yes?"

Phillip nodded.

Without seeming either to approve or disapprove, Mr. DiFrancini took the Trooper back to his counter, where he proceeded to dust it with a flannel cloth and examine it for chips and chinks. Phillip didn't see any, but Mr. DiFrancini seemed concerned by something. Finally, he set the Trooper down and leaned across the counter, his enormous head looming over Phillip like a parade balloon. He kept his voice low. "Now Mrs. Guildenweiser tells me you may have had an unexpected visitor."

Phillip went still. He hadn't thought anyone else was supposed to know. He looked over at Mrs. Guildenweiser, who was back by the door now, sitting with Lara, but she didn't seem at all concerned. She offered a vague and aged wave.

"When did it happen?" asked Mr. DiFrancini.

Phillip thought. It seemed like a long time ago, but his parents had only left last Friday. The Beastie had shown up the following night.

"Three days ago," he said.

"And what makes you think it was him?"

Phillip once again looked over at Mrs. Guildenweiser for help, but she was distracted with Lara now, who was mucking the glass door with her nose.

"The bathtub was dirty," said Phillip. "And there were footprints. I also think it took something."

"What? If I may ask."

Phillip was a little embarrassed to say—"A baseball mitt"—but Mr. DiFrancini's reaction was reassuring. He pressed his lips together and nodded knowingly.

"And you're afraid he might come back, is that it?"

Not afraid, said Phillip's expression.

"But you suspect?"

"Maybe," said Phillip. "I have more mitts." He purposely didn't say how many more, but Mr. DiFrancini seemed to understand. He looked back at the Union Trooper, his brows severely arched with doubt.

"I'm just not sure that's going to be big enough."

He thought for another moment, then lifted his finger to keep Phillip in place while he ducked behind the curtain to his storage room.

It was nothing against Mrs. Guildenweiser, but Phillip was relieved to find that someone else knew about the Beastie, and especially Mr. DiFrancini, who didn't seem the sort of person who put up with foolishness. Phillip peered through the crack in the curtains, but all he could see was the jarful of pencil-thin brushes on the little desk where Mr. DiFrancini liked to touch up his pieces. He glanced at a catalog on the counter. A whole page of Confederate soldiers, and there beside it, his mother's voucher.

Good for one (1) soldier from Mr. DiFrancini's soldier shop.

And now Mr. DiFrancini was back. "Here we are." He stepped through the curtains, but with something in his two hands that Phillip in his wildest imagination would never have thought possible. It was the Union Trooper—exactly the same as the one Phillip had chosen—only it was all bronze, and twice as big. Maybe three times. Maybe four.

Mr. DiFrancini set it down on the counter. "This is more likely to do the trick." He flicked on the desk lamp, and all the details leapt at them in polished bronze: the tangles in the horse's mane, the crossed swords on the cap, the wrinkles in the gloves and boots. Even the spurs had a design on them.

But Phillip didn't understand. This was clearly a statue, not a toy. He looked back at Mrs. Guildenweiser, who was just now coming over to see for herself.

"Oh, yes," she said, while Lara trotted up behind. "Yes, that's very nice."

"But I don't think my mother would let me," said Phillip.

Mrs. Guildenweiser paused, not seeing why not. She referred to the voucher. She spun it around to read, and turned it back to Mr. DiFrancini, who likewise, once he'd put on his glasses, seemed to see no problem.

He looked down at Phillip. "Now, do you have a window in your room?"

Yes, nodded Phillip.

"Does it look out over the park?"

Yes, nodded Phillip.

"You need to stand him in the window—just before bedtime. Make sure there's enough space and that the view is clear. Then if the Beastie does make an appearance, he'll let you know." He tapped the Trooper's shoulder with complete confidence.

Phillip didn't understand.

"The *statues*," Mr. DiFrancini explained. "They're the only ones that he lets see him."

He said this as if Phillip should understand, though in fact Phillip had no idea what Mr. DiFrancini was talking about. The statues? He looked up at Mrs. Guildenweiser, but she too seemed to take the wisdom of the plan for granted. Even the Trooper appeared to approve, with those deep-set eyes set in the distance, poised at any moment to awaken from their squint and give him the signal. How could Phillip say no?

"Would you like me to wrap it, then?"

That night, after putting on his pajamas and brushing his teeth, Phillip did just as Mr. DiFrancini had instructed. He set the Trooper up on the windowsill in his bedroom, look-ing out at the street lamp and down on the park. Then in bed he propped up his pillow so that when he opened his eyes, the Trooper would be the first thing he saw. He tested several times—closing and opening, closing and opening—and every time the Trooper was right there where he should be, standing guard, he and his beaming blue profile slanted against the frame: the crook in his nose, the tuft of his mus-tache, the knot of the kerchief around his neck . . .

. . . And Phillip wouldn't have said he fell asleep. He would have said he was on the *verge* of falling asleep when he heard the familiar sound of the front door clicking shut. He sat straight up. His parents? No. They weren't due un-til tomorrow night. He listened, but all was quiet. He crept out of bed and peeked into the foyer. Lara was asleep on her side like a rug. The front door, still. He turned back to his room, and his breath caught short. The window shade was flat against the sash. The Trooper wasn't there.

Then he saw the tennis ball on the floor, ever so infinitesimally rocking back and forth in the evening breeze. The closet door was open. He got down on his knees and crawled to where he could see inside. The shorter of his two baskets was tipped over and empty, all but for some stray pucks and balls huddled together. The baseball mitts were gone. All of them. Even his gamer.

Clip-clop clip-clop clip-clop. There was a sound outside the window. Phillip went to the sill and looked down just in time to see the Trooper crossing the street. It was very clearly him. He had his sword and his pistol, and he was bronze. The only difference (aside from his size) was that he also had a sack slung over his shoulder, full like a laundry bag, but chunkier. And now he was entering the park.

Phillip ran. He put on his slippers and went as fast as he could. He had to tiptoe over Lara in the foyer and make sure the front door didn't creak too loud, but as soon as he was out in the hall, he raced. He took the stairs so as not to rouse the elevator man, down six smooth banisters and past the snoring doorman. He ran across the sleeping street with all the sleeping cars, and knowing that if his mother saw she would have had a heart attack, he did the one thing he was most supposed not to do. In the middle of the night, wearing nothing but his pajamas and slippers, he entered the park.

In the lamplight up ahead, Phillip could see the pony's

tail just now turning right onto the first bridge. They were headed for the playing fields. Phillip kept running, with shadows trailing him and leading him, and twisting all around him. By the time he made it across the bridge himself, the Trooper was entering the underpass. Phillip could hear the pony's hooves chattering against the arched brick. He followed as fast as he could, past the museum and into the tunnel and the echo of his scuffing slippers.

As he came out the other side, the Trooper was still up ahead, nearing the bank of the turtle pond, still with the sack over his shoulder, but then out of nowhere—

"Pssssst . . ."

Phillip stopped short.

". . . Psssssst!"

The sound was coming from the giant stone needle.

". . . Who is that there?"

It was a girl's voice, with an English accent, but with the lamppost behind her, all Phillip could see was her outline: her long flowing hair, the little bow on top, the puffs at the shoulder of her dress, and the way it ballooned out from her waist like an umbrella. He knew exactly who that was.

"Who are you?" she asked.

The others were there as well. The rabbit in the dresscoat, and the buck-toothed dwarf in the top hat. Even the cat was perched on the bough above the others, lazily swinging its bronze tail like a feather.

"What are you doing here?" asked the girl, her slender polished finger pointing directly at him. "I don't think you're supposed to be." She peered closer, as if *he* were the strange-looking one, all flesh and pajamas and hair. "Who let you in?"

Phillip wasn't sure. He glanced over at the Trooper, who'd stopped not far ahead, beneath a glowing lamppost.

"He took my mitts."

The Trooper looked back in silence, now pinching a black clump from his bronze pouch and stuffing it under his giant mustache.

"But it's so warm?" said the girl. "Who needs mitts?"

"Baseball mitts," said Phillip, indicating the heavy sack hanging from the Trooper's shoulder.

"My, my," clucked the bucked-tooth man. "How many mitts do you have?"

"Eight," said Phillip. "Left."

The buck-toothed man sniffed. "How many hands do you have?"

"Two."

"Then shouldn't two mitts do?"

Clearly the man knew nothing about baseball, but he had a good point just the same.

"They're still mine," said Phillip. He looked accusingly at the Trooper, who for the first time replied in words, his voice low and steady and slightly muffled by his mustache.

"I thought you'd want to see him."

There was a moment of silence. Phillip didn't have to ask whom he was talking about. They all knew.

"Do you?" asked the girl. "Is that what you're doing here?"

Phillip thought. He wouldn't have said so before, but

now that the Trooper had mentioned it, and now that he was actually here, it seemed fairly clear that yes, that *was* what he was doing here.

The Trooper swung the sack around from his shoulder and tipped it open. Out spilled the gloves, one after another, tumbling onto the grass and taking a moment to settle. Phillip counted all eight, including his gamer.

"Shouldn't take long," the Trooper murmured, treating himself to another pinch of bronze tobacco.

A breeze stirred, and a moment later the rabbit's ears flicked to the north side of the field. A distant howl sounded, which might have been more frightening except that it was followed by whoop-whoop. The Cheshire Cat jumped down from its limb and started pacing behind the girl. Phillip could barely see in the moonlight, but over on the far side of the field there was a rustling in the leaves of one of the trees, and now it was moving to the next tree over, like a tight little breeze coming this way. He could clearly see its progress, all the limbs and leaves bowing beneath the weight, shivering, and nodding in its wake. From one tree to the next it rounded the field until right there in front of them a shadow dropped from a low branch and tumbled onto a bench, then up onto the cap of the lamppost, so perfectly balanced and still, it was as if the thing had been perching there the whole time.

He wasn't very big, but with the lamplight underneath him it was hard to make out more—just a dark little figure, with pointed ears on top of his head, and a low swinging arm.

The Trooper stepped his horse back from the mitts to clear

the way, and in another blink the Beastie jumped down and tumbled to an upright stop in front of them. Phillip could see him better now. He wasn't much taller than Phillip, but he was shaped more like a fire hydrant with legs. He was covered from head to toe in dark thick fur, though less so around his calves and feet, which were very large. Had a small potbelly, upon which rested an extra abundance of hair trailing from his chin like a beard. He had a very large mouth, with an equally broad flat forehead, his eyes buried deep beneath his brow, but peering out—two faint glimmers of light, but just enough to show. How familiar he seemed. His appearance was in no way surprising to Phillip, but surprisingly familiar.

The mitts were still all there at his feet. The Beastie picked one up, Phillip's gamer, of course. He sniffed it, and his eyes rolled back in ecstasy. Phillip could tell what he wanted to do, but the Beastie picked up a second mitt instead, the first baseman's. He twisted it backward, stared at it thoughtfully for a moment, then proceeded to stuff the whole thing into his mouth like a giant dumpling. Phillip just stood and watched as the Beastie chewed slowly with a great rolling jaw, and as he did his deep dark eyes slid over beneath his brow. He looked directly at Phillip, grinning, and swallowed with an open gulp. Phillip could hear the glove sliding down the Beastie's throat and landing softly in his belly, which offered a low rumble of contentment.

The Beastie glanced around now. He hadn't realized the others were there. He didn't seem bothered, though. He picked up a third glove, Phillip's raggedy old outfielder's glove, and slipped it back inside the Trooper's sack. He did the same with the pitcher's mitt, then all the rest from seasons gone by—he gathered them up like groceries and stuffed them in until the only one remaining now was Phillip's gamer. Phillip wouldn't have blamed him if he'd eaten it right there, it looked so soft and delicious. But he didn't. And he didn't put it in the sack, either. He simply dropped it on the grass. He was leaving it behind, kindly.

The rest he slung up over his shoulder, then he started off across the path, running and tumbling and offering little humming grunts as his good-bye. He started around the Turtle Pond. There weren't so many trees that way, so he kept rolling and jumping along the bank, all the way out onto the rocks beneath Belvedere Castle. He scrambled up and slipped inside the lowest window, a black sliver in the stone.

"You should go," whispered Alice from behind.

The Trooper agreed. "Sun'll be up soon."

The rabbit consulted his pocket watch; it was true. So Phillip went and grabbed his one remaining mitt, and the only one he needed really, and the Trooper lifted him up onto the pony. Phillip felt like a feather on his arm. He sat up front, holding onto the mane for balance. The statues all raised their hands in farewell, the Trooper tapped his heels, and the pony started them away, down the path, under the bridge, over the bridge, and out.

BUZZ BISSINGER
The Goodbye

I N THE LATE 1950s my parents, escaping the Upper
East Side of New York that was the de rigueur repository of virtually all their friends, made their move to Central Park West and Eighty-eighth Street. The rent was about
two hundred dollars a month for a seven-room apartment
overlooking the park with four bedrooms and four baths.
My father, in advertising and much like Don Draper wore a
soft-brimmed brown hat and smoked like a chimney and
wasn't above a few drinks at lunch and came home each
night whipsawed by control freak clients, thought the rent
was reasonable. So did my mother, who sold bras at
Macy's, a labor-intensive act with far too much anatomical
requirements, before moving to Chiquita, where bananas
were far less prickly.

I was close to three at the time, so my knowledge of the
move was quite scant, particularly since I had taken a vow of

silence on the basis that there was not nearly as much to say in life as most people thought. My sister was five. She talked incessantly, and it is safe to say her ambivalence about me was abundant when she tried to drown me in the bathtub.

My parents moved to the ninth-floor apartment because it had more space than the cramped East Side digs. My mother really chose it for the view. The living room and my sister's and parents' bedroom all had picture window views of Central Park. My room was on the other side of the apartment. It was so dark you could watch a movie in daylight without pulling down the shades. My view was the abyss of a courtyard where it was always entertaining to throw wet toilet paper bombs out the window and hear them splat until the superintendent said he was going to come upstairs and kick my ass if I did it again. As I got older, my eye was naturally drawn to the charred outline of a window across the way where a tenant had allegedly set herself on fire. For some reason, I turned out to be quite morose and melancholic.

I was, however, allowed free visiting privileges into the other rooms. I cannot say with certainty when I became fully conscious of the park, but my initial interaction with it was from the living room. There was a white couch next to the picture window of a very strange and slippery texture. If you did not sit the right way, you were liable to slip off, so I clung to the corner with my feet up for extra balance.

Looking down into Central Park was like inserting yourself into the best soul of the city that in the sixties was convulsing with garbage strikes and teacher strikes and race riots. My mother loved John Lindsay. I think every woman over the age of five loved John Lindsay. Come to think of it, so did every man. He was handsome and passionate and articulate, but as a mayor the city simply swallowed him and sank further and further into decline. Maybe in retrospect he should have been a porn star.

For much of that period, Central Park seemed to be the only place that held hope, however wobbly because of its dilapidation. Buildings rose and fell and rose again in the ever-shifting city, even during the difficult times. Mayors came and went, the great disappointment of Lindsay giving way to the oddly enduring impishness of Abe Beame in the 1970s, as the city teetered on bankruptcy, to the infectiousness of Ed Koch in the 1980s. There was little sustained consistency, this sense that the city could still explode at any second. But Central Park stayed as it was, or mostly as it was. It was badly in need of a haircut and a shave, garbage cans needed to be emptied more than once a year, and the dangers of the park at night became manna for the *New York Daily News* and *New York Post*.

Central Park was still the single greatest city-planning feat of New York and perhaps any city in the world. It also became the one egalitarian place in Manhattan, young next to old, aimless next to ambitious, homeless wearing the Sunday *New York Times* next to the nobility of Fifth Avenue reading the *New York Times*. I often wondered what it would be like if they switched.

Central Park was where I played baseball and football. It brought me peace and pride. It brought me wonder and

conjured up dreams. All that I wanted in life, all that anybody could want in life, was somehow there, sight, sense,
smell, sensation. Every step I took always felt new, yet carried the shadow of memory and irreplaceable youth, my
mother and my father, the great wars of Sunday softball
games, the endless people watching, the food stands where
hot dogs drowned in what looked like dishwater that only
made them taste better, the fine art of dodging dogshit.

It was only later, on the cusp of my fifties, I learned there
was something even Central park could not overcome.

From the age of five on I remember going into the park almost every weekend, taking the entrance across the street
and going down the ramp holding the hands of my father or
my mother. I remember the bridle path where you could ride
horses. I remember moving through clumps of trees and
little hillocks of rocks, my only real interaction with nature
in an urban environment until I was a Boy Scout and went
camping in the great wilds of North Jersey. I remember the
Reservoir, which always made me a little nervous because
this was the drinking water for at least part of the city and
God knows what was in it.

There were very few joggers then in the 1960s because
there mercifully was no concept of health. Maybe it was just
my parents' friends, but everybody ate bloodred roast beef
sandwiches with the works from one of the plethora of local
delis. Everybody smoked and drank, laughter rolling from
glasses filled with Scotch instead of Crate and Barrel goblets

of white wine and disgusting crudités of broccoli and carrots and cauliflower.

Most of all, I remember the annual Sunday ritual of the Great Lawn occupying the park between Seventy-ninth and Eighty-fifth streets. There was a paved circle on the perimeter, lined with benches where people read the Sunday *Times* or *Herald Tribune,* or sunned themselves with eyes closed in the mirth of the sun. It was the baseball diamonds edging into the lawn that mesmerized me the most, émigrés from Puerto Rico who, when they weren't arguing or threatening to kill each other with a baseball bat, played a mean game of softball. The grass had been rubbed out long ago and was dirt, so fielding a grounder always carried the risk of death because of a bad hop. Then there was the crack of ball against bat and a laser shot over the left fielder's head and the left fielder chasing in pursuit and the ensuing chaos of players from another game across the way screaming at the left fielder to get the hell off their field. The hitter meanwhile rounded first and second and third in a tight pattern and then went for home to bugles of noise from his teammates telling him to slide and bugles of noise from opponents telling the relay man to make the throw home. The play was always close even if it wasn't. One side said the batter was safe. The other side said the runner was out, which then led to a loud argument in Spanish that usually took as long as the game itself.

I could have stayed for hours watching the operatic ritual unfold. But then my father and mother took my hand again. We made our way to the greater tranquillity of the East Side. We went by the Metropolitan Museum of Art. My mother always wanted to go inside. My father and I outnumbered her, so sometimes we would go to the old movie theater on Madison to catch a film. Or the opposite direction to the Madison Deli on Eighty-sixth where the sandwiches were as big as my head and the Russian dressing and coleslaw dripped down my chin in joyous piggery.

In 1972 I left New York to go to the University of Pennsylvania in Philadelphia. I became a newspaper reporter after that and then a nonfiction author and writer for *Vanity Fair.* I moved about the country—Norfolk, St. Paul, Milwaukee, Texas, back to Philadelphia—but Central Park never left me. My parents still lived in the same apartment, so I always felt I had New York bragging rights. I still considered it my home, and whenever I was there, now a father with three children and sometimes a wife depending on which marriage, we always made the loop of the Great Lawn.

I could not imagine life without Central Park. I could not imagine waking up and making a cup of coffee and going into the living room and not staring out the window into that panorama. It was just as spectacular at night, the twinkling lights of the grand concrete dowagers of Fifth Avenue across the way. I spent hours wondering what went on inside those windows. I imagined fanciful and perfect lives—girls from Brearley and Spence in cotton nightgowns having pillow fights before dropping acid, and parents instructing the maid to give them all a kiss good night as they went off to Swifty's or Lutèce, and the girls now smoking grass.

Often at night, my father and I would sit in soft-backed chairs opposite each other in the living room flanked by the picture window of the park. We talked about our lives; the glasses of Scotch came closer and closer to the brim with each iteration until we both agreed we were too drunk to make any coherent sense and needed to sleep it off.

I never felt closer to my family than I did in those moments, even in the throes of inebriation. I thought we would last forever. In a way I cannot quite explain, I felt a sense of immortality because Central Park was immortal, that everything would always stay the same.

Sometime in the spring of 2001, my mother's physical and mental health, which had been on a descending slope for several years, took a radical turn for the worse. She had mysterious fainting spells, one time falling off the sidewalk on Fifth Avenue into the street before a Good Samaritan saved her. She was hospitalized at Lenox Hill, where neurologists pecked and pawed and knew something was severely wrong but could not pinpoint the cause. Maybe it was Parkinson's. Maybe it was Alzheimer's. Seventy-four years old, she became increasingly disoriented and unable to process. For every day of the two weeks she was there, my father kept vigil. He arrived at nine in the morning and left at eight at night, only exiting the room to go out for lunch. He was seventy-five, and his protectiveness of her was not only touching; it reinforced in a more powerful way than ever before how deeply they were in love, fifty-plus years of marriage sealed into an unbreakable companionship.

She came home more disoriented than ever. Her acuity had been the best part of her, but now the world seemed fuzzy and foggy. She began to lose her ability to walk and spent most of her days in bed reading the same article in *Time* magazine over and over again. She became more dependent on my father than ever. He was a man prone to frustration, and he was frustrated by what was happening to her, but he worried constantly.

Until June of 2001 when I received my weekly call from him. "Just checking in" was the way he always started the conversation in an upbeat lilt, to which I generally responded with some bitch and moan about work until he finally decreed that I would have exactly five minutes to bitch and moan about work until I was required to turn to something else. But this call was different:

He had just been diagnosed with acute myeloid leukemia and was subsequently hospitalized. On the taxi ride to Mt. Sinai he let out a wail and said he was scared. It was the first time he had ever shown such vulnerability. I took his hand and tried to console him, but I was utterly unprepared for the role reversal that inevitably takes place when your father becomes sick and you, the son, become the caregiver.

My mother did not understand what was going on. She had no clue that he had cancer in all likelihood fatal. But one day we did take her to see him. She was in a wheel-chair. My valiant sister pushed her the whole way, and we went through the park, transversing the Great Lawn from west to east. The park was in its glory thanks to the work of the Central Park Conservancy, lush and green, trees spreading their wings with proud majesty. Even though this was a walk I had made a thousand times, everything felt fresh and alive. Until we reached the entrance of Mt. Sinai, and I felt the dread of knowing my father was dying and the inability of my mother to comprehend it.

After being filled with chemotherapy through a port that had been placed just below the shoulder, he came home. He fought valiantly. He refused to accept that he even had leukemia, until there was a recurrence. He went back into the hospital. He knew it was over. We both knew it was over. I could offer no reassurance now, only the silence of fate.

He died in October of 2001.

My mother had collapsed mentally and physically. She could not walk. She was incontinent. She often called out to my father, thinking he was coming home at any second or that he was still there in the apartment.

My sister and I groped for ways to connect her with the things about New York she had loved. So almost every day we took her to Central Park in her wheelchair. We parked it near a bench. We always picked a spot in walking distance of a hot dog stand. She still loved to eat so we all got hot dogs and sodas. The sun fell on her face and she felt tranquil in those moments, the place of New York she loved the best among so many.

We took her to a neurologist at Columbia Presbyterian. He believed she might be suffering from hydrocephalus, an abnormal buildup of fluid in the brain. A shunt was put in to relieve the pressure. It worked momentarily—she was even able to walk a little bit—but then she lapsed and had to be hospitalized. The shunt became infected. Sepsis set in, leading to liver failure.

Four months after my father, my mother died in March.

The apartment was rent stabilized. My parents were paying $2,700 a month, an obscene deal in New York given the location. The landlord immediately raised it to $7,000, then $10,000. My sister and I could not keep it. The hideous process of emptying out took place—years and years of the accumulation of furniture and clothing and knickknacks and family papers.

I was the only one there when the apartment had been finally swept clean. I puttered about, going into each of the rooms before ending up in the living room. I stared out the picture window. Central Park unfolded like a magic carpet. I could see the joggers and the dog walkers. I could see the Guggenheim and the spires of Fifth Avenue.

I lingered for another second or two. Then I went to the front door and opened it and heard the click of the lock for the final time. Central Park beckoned. It always beckoned. But like so much else, the loss of my parents, the childhood so distant, the memories now nostalgic, it would never be mine again.

DOUG BLONSKY
Epilogue

M Y PERSONAL INVESTMENT in working with landscape started at a very young age. But in the beginning, mine was not a labor of love. My father used to have me work in our yard each weekend, and once every spring, mulch would arrive by way of an eighteen-wheel truck that would unload its burden at the base of our driveway. I would spend hours carefully spreading the nutrient-rich mixture across the thirsty plant beds. This once-endless toil eventually turned from dread to discovery as the earth began to teach me the lessons born of my efforts. It was during this time that I first made the connection between landscape and man.

Years later, in 1980, I visited Central Park on a field trip from the University of Delaware with my Landscape Design Studio class. I remember being dropped off by our bus on Fifth Avenue and Ninetieth Street like it was yesterday. Our

assignment was to walk, look, study, and, through sketch-
ing, express how we felt about the experience.

We walked south on the bridle path; graffiti covered
most surfaces, the pathways were eroded and rats were
equal in number to people, and the woods were filled with
as many dead trees as live. Bridge 24 was rusted, missing
most of its ornamental cast iron, and covered with graffiti
as well. We continued south to the Great Lawn, which had
barely any grass and which I would later learn was referred
to as the "Great Dust Bowl," because when the wind blew
you could hardly breathe.. Turtle Pond was filled not only
with garbage but also with many dead fish; the stench was
awful. Looking up at Belvedere Castle, we saw yet another
boarded-up facility, covered with graffiti and surrounded by
litter, the granite parapet walls crumbling. I discovered years
afterward that three ornamental loggias were completely
missing.

Needless to say, our assignment never got completed that
day and we retreated to a pub somewhere on Madison
Avenue. Little did I know then that I would go on to get a
degree in landscape architecture and come back to the park
five short years later.

Those of us drawn to landscape design have a deep appreciation for its legacy and integral role in the evolution
of man. No one understood this better than the founding
fathers of Central Park, Olmsted and Vaux. Like all great
masters they recognized what they needed to build was not
a thing to behold, but an experience. This is why their

masterpiece continues to endure more than a century and a half later. But this was not always the case.

By the mid-twentieth century, this Garden of Eden for New Yorkers was almost lost. Its once-tranquil landscape no longer provided an escape from the urban jungle that had sprung up around it. There was still hope, however, because the absence of its former bounty was clearly felt. In 1980, a small group of dedicated New Yorkers banded together with a single goal: to restore Central Park and ensure that its essential purpose endured. They became the caretakers of the very heart of our city.

Now, more than thirty years since it began as the curator of this masterpiece, the Central Park Conservancy has learned to accommodate the modern demands of a growing audience of over forty million annual visitors. I have spent my career helping this incredible organization restore Central Park to a point that perhaps even Olmsted and Vaux never dreamed possible. While most of my time at the Conservancy has been spent in operations, design, and planning, now, as president, my focus has shifted to fund-raising and making sure we have the resources to support the forty-two million dollars it takes every year to keep the park the world-class cultural institution that it is today. In total, the Conservancy has raised nearly 600 million dollars, with over 450 million coming from generous New Yorkers.

The connection that visitors make with the park's original intent as a scenic retreat from urban life has never been more real than it is today. Our staff understands this, and now exploration and discovery are common themes addressed in the Conservancy's strategic plan. The necessity of maintaining the delicate balance between man and nature, art and discovery, so clearly understood by Olmsted and Vaux over 150 years ago, has been tested to the near-ruin of Central Park, and our ability to educate visitors about that chapter in the park's history is a critical part of ensuring its survival. Our mandate as New Yorkers and as lovers of Central Park is clear: We can never take Central Park for granted and it can never be allowed to go back to what it was before the founding of its guardian, the Central Park Conservancy. I feel honored to be a part of the success of Central Park and am confident that the park's future is secure, because we all know the importance that Central Park holds for New York and the world.

IMAGINE there's no Central Park . . .

In Walker Percy's novel *The Moviegoer*, Binx Bolling frequents movies because they provide him with the "treasurable moments" so often too absent from his real life. So, too, do we seek and find such moments in Central Park.

Ask people what they love most about New York and the majority will name the same thing: Central Park. Ask what all of those people love most about Central Park, and you will almost never get two alike answers. Such is the vastness, the diversity, the wonder of this place that plays so many different roles to so many different kinds of people.

Central Park is like baseball in the sense that it continues to change but remains, in essence, very much the same. There are many paradoxes of the park; it divides, as it does physically (separating East Side from West Side), but also unites us, just as it somehow simultaneously defines and defies the city. We often feel more at home in the park than in our erstwhile homes. We go to be alone and to be with others, seeking solitude and community. It's where we go to pray and to play, to meditate and celebrate.

My first two anthologies were portraits of people—coaches and brothers—and yet this book, about a place, a *public* place, feels even more personal and private, intimate and emotional, so tied in, so often, to what matters most.

Anthology is defined as a bouquet of flowers. I hope that you have enjoyed the array here.

Gratitude must be paid. To my estimable editor, Anton Mueller, and wonderful publisher George Gibson. Without the two of you, this book would not exist. And to everyone at Bloomsbury, including: Nikki Baldauf, Murray Berman, Alona Fryman, Carrie Majer, and Rachel Mannheimer.

My profound appreciation to Adrian Benepe, commissioner of the New York City Department of Parks & Recreation, and to Douglas Blonsky, president of the Central Park Conservancy. Your support, from the outset, has been critical, and my admiration for the work that you do is immense. Vickie Karp, director of public affairs at the Department of Parks & Recreation, you have been a trusty secret weapon, and I'm agog at all that you do (and the apropos anagram of your name is not lost on me).

Thank you to Dan Daly, Dena Libner, Sara Cedar Miller, Nicole Sexton, Norma Soto, Kate Spellman, Rebecca Stern, Myra Sylman, and to everyone else at the Parks Department and Conservancy, all of the people of the park who make everything possible.

Special thanks to Elizabeth Kurtz, whose assistance has been invaluable.

And to Frederick Law Olmsted and Calvert Vaux, we are perpetually, eternally in your debt.

ABOUT THE CONTRIBUTORS

Paul Auster is the bestselling author of sixteen novels (including *Sunset Park*, *Invisible*, *Man in the Dark*, *Travels in the Scriptorium*, *The Brooklyn Follies*, *Timbuktu*, *Oracle Night*, and *The New York Trilogy*) and four screenplays (*The Inner Life of Martin Frost*, *Lulu on the Bridge*, *Smoke*, and *Blue in the Face*, which he co-directed with Wayne Wang), as well as several translations and works of nonfiction. In 2006, Auster was inducted into the American Academy of Arts and Letters. He also won Spain's most prestigious prize for literature—the Premio Principe de Asturias de las Letras—in 2006. Among other awards he has won are the Commandeur de l'Ordre des Arts et des Lettres, the Prix Médicis for the best foreign novel published in France (1992), and the Silver Bear from the Berlin Film Festival for *Smoke* (1995). His work has been translated into forty languages.

Thomas Beller, an avid basketball player, lives with his family in New York and New Orleans. His books include two works of fiction, *Seduction Theory* and *The Sleep-Over Artist*, and a collection of personal essays, *How to Be a Man*. His stories have appeared in the *St. Ann's Review*, *Ploughshares*, the *New Yorker*, *Elle*, and *Best American Short Stories*. He has edited numerous anthologies, including *Lost and Found: Stories from New York* and *Before and After: Stories from New York*. He was founder and for twenty years co-editor of the literary journal and press *Open City*, and founded the literary Web site mrbellersneighborhood.com. He teaches at Tulane University.

Adrian Benepe, has worked for more than thirty-two years protecting and enhancing New York City's natural and historic beauty. He has continued this effort as commissioner of the New York City Department of Parks & Recreation, appointed by Mayor Michael R. Bloomberg on January 25, 2002.

After graduating from Middlebury College in Vermont, he became a member of the first corps of Parks & Recreation's Urban Park Rangers in 1979. He then served in several positions including director of natural resources and horticulture (overseeing scores of restoration projects in the city's wetlands and forests), director of art and antiquities (in charge of the city's conservation and interpretation of thirteen hundred statues and monuments and twenty-three historic house museums), and vice president for issues and public affairs for the Municipal Art Society. From 1990 to 1993, Commissioner Benepe was the director of the Annual Fund & Major Gifts for the New York Botanical Garden in the Bronx, where he expanded his knowledge of plants, trees, and children's education. At the Garden, he co-founded the "Holiday Garden Railway" exhibition.

After six years in the nonprofit sector, he returned to Parks & Recreation in January 1996 as the Manhattan borough commissioner, where he managed Manhattan's green infra-structure of more than three hundred parks, playgrounds, and malls, and helped found the Fort Tryon Park Trust, a public-private partnership for the historic park and its Heather Garden. He served in that position until promoted to commissioner of the Department of Parks & Recreation, where he now oversees the operation of over 29,000 acres and nearly 4,000 properties including over 1,000 play-grounds, 600 ballfields, 600 tennis courts, 63 swimming pools, 35 recreation centers, 14 miles of beach, and over 2.5 million street and park trees.

Adrian Benepe holds a B.A. in English literature from Middlebury College and a master's degree in journalism from Columbia University, where he was awarded a Pulit-zer Fellowship.

Buzz Bissinger is a Pulitzer Prize winner and the author of three bestselling nonfiction books, including the American classic *Friday Night Lights*. He is a contributing editor at *Vanity Fair* and the sports columnist for the *Daily Beast*. His parents lived on Central Park West for nearly forty-five years, and he grew up there.

Douglas Blonsky is the senior executive responsible for managing and overseeing all operations for Central Park. He is a registered landscape architect and a member of the American Society of Landscape Architecture. He is presi-dent of the Central Park Conservancy, the not-for-profit organization responsible for managing and maintaining

Central Park, one of New York City's most valuable resources. In addition to holding the position of president, he was appointed to the position of Central Park Administrator in 1998 when the Conservancy formalized its partnership with the City of New York by signing a historic management contract that officially made the Conservancy responsible for the park's management and operation. Since 1985, he has helped lead the park through the transition from its derelict condition of the early '80s to its position today as one of the most magnificent and emulated parks in the world. The Conservancy has successfully raised and spent over 600 million dollars on the restoration and maintenance of Central Park, $435 million of which was raised from private philanthropy, providing thirty-eight million annual visitors a beautiful and unique experience.

Bill Buford is a former staff writer and fiction editor at the *New Yorker*, and the founding editor of *Granta*. He is the author of *Among the Thugs* and *Heat: An Amateur's Adventures as a Kitchen Slave, Line Cook, Pasta Maker, and Apprentice to a Dante-Quoting Butcher in Tuscany* and is completing a book about becoming a French cook.

Susan Cheever has written fifteen books, including a biography of Bill Wilson, the co-founder of Alcoholics Anonymous, and a memoir about her father, the writer John Cheever. She has taught at Columbia and Yale and currently teaches at Bennington and the New School. She lives in New York City with her family.

Ben Dolnick is the author of *Zoology* and *You Know Who You Are*. He lives in Brooklyn, New York.

Jonathan Safran Foer is the author of *Eating Animals* and the novels *Everything Is Illuminated* and *Extremely Loud and Incredibly Close*. His work has received numerous awards and has been translated into thirty-six languages. He lives in Brooklyn, New York.

Adam Gopnik has been a staff writer at the *New Yorker* for the past twenty-five years and is the author, most recently, of *The Steps Across the Water* and *The Table Comes First*, a collection of his essays about eating.

Born in New York City in 1965, **Brooks Hansen** is the author of one memoir and six novels, including *The Chess Garden* and most recently *John the Baptizer*, for which he was named a Guggenheim fellow. Also a screenwriter, he lives and teaches in Carpinteria, California, with his wife and two children.

Mark Helprin, born in 1947 and soon transported from the now nonexistent Doctor's Hospital in Yorkville to an apartment overlooking Central Park, is the author of, among other works, *Winter's Tale* and *A Soldier of the Great War*.

British-born **Donald Knowler** has spent a lifetime in journalism, working for newspapers that include the *Independent* in London and, in broadcasting, the BBC. He lived in

Africa and North America during the 1970s and '80s, when he worked as a correspondent for a news agency, and has now made his home in Australia. He currently works as an editor and environmental journalist for the *Mercury*, in Hobart, Tasmania.

David Michaelis, the author of two national bestsellers, *N.C. Wyeth* (1998) and *Schulz and Peanuts* (2007), is at work on a new biography of Eleanor Roosevelt.

Francine Prose is a novelist and critic whose latest book, the novel *My New American Life*, was published by Harper in May 2011. Her previous books include the novels *Goldengrove*, *A Changed Man*, and *Blue Angel*, which was a finalist for the 2001 National Book Award, and the nonfiction *New York Times* bestseller *Reading Like a Writer: A Guide for People Who Love Books and for Those Who Want to Write Them* and *Anne Frank: The Book, The Life, the Afterlife.* Her articles and essays have appeared in the *New Yorker*, *Harper's*, the *Atlantic*, *Condé Nast Traveler*, *ARTnews*, *Parkett*, *Modern Painters*, and the *New York Times Magazine.* She is the recipient of numerous grants and awards, among them the Dayton Literary Peace Prize, the Edith Wharton Achievement Award for Literature, Guggenheim and Fulbright fellowships, and is a past president of PEN American Center. She lives in New York City.

Nathaniel Rich is the author of two novels: *The Mayor's Tongue* and the forthcoming *Odds Against Tomorrow*.

John Burnham Schwartz is the author of the acclaimed novels *The Commoner, Claire Marvel, Bicycle Days,* and *Reservation Road,* which was made into a motion picture based on his screenplay. His latest novel, *Northwest Corner,* was published in the summer of 2011. His books have been translated into more than twenty languages, and his writing has appeared in many publications, including the *New Yorker* and the *New York Times.* A past winner of the Lyndhurst Foundation Award for mastery in the art of fiction, Schwartz has taught at the Iowa Writers' Workshop, Harvard University, and Sarah Lawrence College, and is currently literary director of the Sun Valley Writers' Conference. He lives in Brooklyn, New York, with his wife, Aleksandra Crapanzano, and their son, Garrick.

Susan Sheehan is the author of eight books, including the Pulitzer Prize–winning *Is There No Place on Earth for Me?* She has been a staff writer for the *New Yorker* for over forty-five years and a contributing writer for *Architectural Digest* for fifteen years.

Colson Whitehead was born and raised in Manhattan. His first novel, *The Intuitionist,* concerned intrigue in the Department of Elevator Inspectors and was a finalist for the PEN/Hemingway Award and a winner of the Quality Paperback Book Club's New Voices Award. Subsequent novels, including *John Henry Days* (2001), *The Colossus of New York* (2003), *Apex Hides the Hurt* (2006), and *Sag Harbor* (2009), have been finalists for or received such honors as the National Book Critics Circle Award, the *Los Angeles Times* Fiction Award, the Pulitzer Prize, the Young Lions Fiction Award, the Anisfield-Wolf Book Award, the PEN/Faulkner Award, and the *New York Times* Notable Book of the Year distinction. Whitehead's reviews, essays, and fiction have appeared in a number of publications, such as the *New York Times,* the *New Yorker, New York* magazine, *Harper's,* and *Granta.* He has also received a MacArthur Fellowship, a Whiting Writers' Award, and a fellowship at the Cullman Center for Scholars and Writers.

Alec Wilkinson has been a writer at the *New Yorker* since 1980. Before that he was a policeman in Wellfleet, Massachusetts, and before that he was a rock-and-roll musician. He has written nine books—two memoirs, two collections of essays, two works of reporting, and three biographical portraits. Among his honors and awards are a Robert F. Kennedy Book Award, a Lyndhurst Prize, and a Guggenheim Fellowship.

Marie Winn is the author of thirteen books, including *Red-Tails in Love: Pale Male's Story—A True Wildlife Drama in Central Park* and *The Plug-In Drug: Television, Computers, and Family Life.* Formerly a contributor to the *Wall Street Journal* and the *New York Times Magazine,* she has also translated plays by Vaclav Havel for performance at the Public Theater in New York. Her Web site, www.mariewinn.com, has frequent updates on Central Park's flora and fauna.